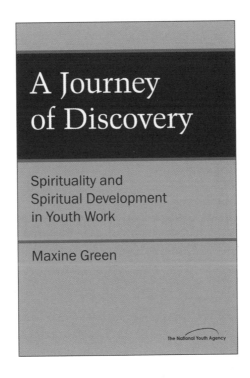

A Journey of Discovery

Spirituality and
Spiritual Development
in Youth Work

Maxine Green

The National Youth Agency

This report builds on a consultation document commissioned by the Department for Education and Skills and prepared by The National Youth Agency. The NYA is grateful to the DfES for its ongoing support of this work. Any views expressed are not necessarily those of the DfES or individuals working within it.

department for
education and skills
creating opportunity, releasing potential, achieving excellence

Extracts from Inspire Too (Scripture Union) used with permission. May not be reproduced without permission in writing from the author and Frontier Youth Trust.

Published July 2006 by

The National Youth Agency

Eastgate House, 19–23 Humberstone Road, Leicester LE5 3GJ.
Tel: 0116 242 7350. Fax: 0116 242 7444.
E-mail: nya@nya.org.uk   Website: www.nya.org.uk

Contents

Foreword	v
Introduction and overview of process	vii
1 The historical and faith context to the subject	1
2 What is spirituality?	5
3 What is spiritual development?	18
4 What is the role of spirituality and spiritual development in youth work?	23
Historical continuity	23
National Occupational Standards	24
Young people's developmental stage	25
The role of the youth worker	27
The 'subversive'/enriching role of spirituality in youth work	29
Preparing young people to be canny about spiritual matters	30
Negative spirituality	31
Broad observations on the above threads	31
5 Key areas for the field arising from this debate	33
How to provide opportunities for young people to explore their spirituality	33
Role of faith communities in developing spirituality	36
What spiritual development means in a secular/statutory setting	37
Spirituality and spiritual development in other organisations	38
Spiritual process and learning outcomes	39
Social justice, social action and spirituality	39
6 Conclusions	41
Appendix 1 Contribution of people with faith to informal education and youth work	42
Appendix 2 The Golden Rule	45
Appendix 3 Faith/spiritual development theories	46
Appendix 4 Spectrum model	50
Appendix 5 National Occupational Standards	51
Appendix 6 Newton's developmental stages	52
Appendix 7 Frontier Youth Trust's ways of working with spirituality	53
Appendix 8 Further definitions of spirituality	55
Appendix 9 Contacts and Resources	58
Appendix 10 Respondees to consultation	68
Appendix 11 Foreword to original consultation document and questions	71
Questions relating to the whole report	72
Bibliography	73

Acknowledgments

I am extremely grateful to all the people who have had conversations with me about spirituality and spiritual development and have in this way made contributions to this paper. I have been very enriched by these discussions and by the importance people have given this subject, and hope that I have interpreted people's thoughts fairly.

I am also aware that this is an ambitious project and that this paper is bound to be partial and fall short. I sincerely hope that people will continue to come forward with new ideas and information so that this subject is treated with the respect and weight that it deserves.

The responses to the initial consultation paper were very thought provoking and considered. A list of those who responded can be found in Appendix 10. I have aimed to reflect the key areas mentioned in this second paper although there is some frustration in not being able to enter into important areas of debate at depth.

In particular I would like to thank the Frontier Youth Trust and Nigel Pimlott for allowing me to use extracts from the publication *Inspire Too* (Frontier Youth Trust 2005) and The Religious Society of Friends for their comprehensive work on spiritual development.

Also, Trudi Newton, Chandu Christian, Tim Clapton, The Inter Faith Network for the United Kingdon for permission to use the extract from *Connect* and The Infed network (www.infed.org), Valdosta State University (http://chiron.valdosta.edu/whuitt/col/regsys/maslow.html), Spectrum and *Youth and Policy*.

Maxine Green
July 2006

Foreword by Bishop Roger Sainsbury

In my introductory letter to the 2005 consultation paper I said: 'The aim of the final paper will be to clarify the present place of spirituality and spiritual development in youth work and to inform professional reflection, policy and practice.' Appendix 10 shows we have had a wide response to our consultation paper and, although Maxine Green reports 'some frustration in not being able to enter into important areas of debate at depth', I believe this report will prove to be a very important document in clarifying the place of spirituality and spiritual development in youth work.

Recent events have shown how important a right understanding of spirituality is, both globally and nationally, particularly for young people. At an inter-faith reception at the Foreign Office in June 2006, reflecting on the global conflicts in the world, the Under Secretary of State Lord Triesman's speech had numerous references to spirituality and its importance for young people. In the House of Lords debate on the Education Bill Bishop George Cassidy quoted the recommendation in The Church of England *Faithful Cities* report: 'The spiritual wellbeing of young people must be an essential part of Youth Matters strategy and implementation.' Lord Melvyn Bragg, a patron of The NYA, when asked at the 2006 Hay Festival what piece of literature could have the greatest influence for good on young people in the new millennium replied, in his opinion, the words of Jesus in the Beatitudes greatly loved by Gandhi – 'Blessed are the poor in spirit; Blessed are those who hunger and thirst to see right prevail; Blessed are the peacemakers.'

Our consultation paper stated: 'Having a voice, challenging discrimination and disadvantage has always been part of the youth work agenda'. In the Make Poverty History campaign, in which thousands of young have been involved, the words of the Chief Rabbi Jonathan Sacks on spirituality and service have been very important: 'We must speak the silent cry of those who today suffer from want, hunger, disease, powerlessness and lack of freedom.' Tariq Ramadan, a plenary speaker at the December 2005 NYA Conference on Muslim Youth Work, picks up the same theme of spirituality and service in his recent book on Western Muslims: 'Muslim Spirituality teaches us fragility, effort and service.'

We are very grateful to Maxine Green for her sensitivity and hard work in writing this report and we hope that it will assist youth workers, other professionals involved with young people, faith leaders and politcans continue the debate that our consultation began.

Yours sincerely

[signature]

Bishop Roger Sainsbury – Chair, The National Youth Agency

References

Faithful Cities Church House Publishing [2006]

The Dignity of Difference Jonathan Sacks, Continuum [2002]

Western Muslims and The Future of Islam Tariq Ramadan, Oxford University Press [2005]

Introduction

This document has been produced by The National Youth Agency with the support of the Department for Education and Skills (DfES) in response to considerable, informed interest in the field. It aims to identify the key areas relating to spirituality and spiritual development and youth work and to undertake an initial exploration of some of the issues relating to them.

The purpose of the document is to facilitate and encourage discussion and to map the territory to enable further debate so that there is more clarity leading to positive informed professional views on this important area.

True to the nature and complexity of the subject it is not desirable to produce a definitive document with guidelines or guidance. However, The NYA and the DfES hope that the document will act as a positive starting point for organisations and individuals to use in developing specific policies and improving practice.

Overview of process

1. **Interest in Spirituality and Spiritual Development in Youth Work**

The National Youth Agency and the Department for Education and Skills have noticed that this area of work has become increasingly questioned and discussed over the last few years. Although there is a reasonable body of information relating to aspects of this work there has been little attempt to produce an overview. This is partly because it is an extremely broad and complex area and partly because there are individuals and organisations with huge investment in this work, in particular major religions. Faith communities expressing their spirituality have also been identified as major influences in social cohesion and community development and stability. A further dimension is the sensitive dynamic between the secular and spiritual debates and how a profession which is now focused within social sciences can have a 'mystical' dimension.

This document endeavours to chart a course between these complexities and cannot satisfy all parties. In an overview it is not possible to go into the various debates in full, or to arrive at a 'party line' or a professional stance. Rather, the aim is to raise various areas for continuing debate and exploration; to put forward the broad impact of spirituality and spiritual development in youth work and to identify the opportunities and threats that this brings to the profession.

2. **Consultation process**

The consultation process started with research during 2004 and 2005 which included desk research and interviews with organisations, groups and individuals. Young people from different faiths and no faith were interviewed in groups and individually. The researcher was also able to draw on her experience in this work over the past 30 years which includes living in the Middle East for ten years, studying social anthropology, working in a large faith organisation at a national level and a vibrant interest in inter faith work. Following the research phase a consultation paper was written which went out to the field. Copies were sent out using The NYA's contacts, it was publicised in *Young People Now* and available both on the website and in paper form. Written responses were welcomed and there was a series of consultations in different parts of the country to get feedback. The responses and feedback have been used to expand the original consultation paper into the present document.

Overall, the feedback to the document was very positive, in particular, that The NYA and the DfES had attempted to address this area which was so complex and potentially problematic. A digest of the issues, identified by the field as needing additional focus or input in the final document, is outlined below in no order of importance:

1. The importance of this debate
    • Inevitably those who responded thought this area was important and gave detailed information about the whole role of spirituality in the youth work curriculum.

2. The participation of young people in the debate and the work
    • Respondents were looking for more of the direct voice of young people in any further publication and wanted them to take part in conferences etc.

3. Explicit engagement with faith and philosophical organisations
    • The need to give the main faiths and other organisations (eg the British Humanist Association) an opportunity to detail their policy and practice with young people.
    • The importance of including the atheist/agnostic philosophies in the debate.

4. Clarification and more information about the transcendental part of spirituality – contact with the 'other' in addition to the work in the paper on the 'self actualisation/humanising' role
    • Some people said that there is no such thing as 'secular spirituality', the transcendental contact with the 'other' needs to be more explicit in the debate.

5. Information about negative spirituality – spiritual abuse, fundamentalism etc
    • People were aware of the destructiveness of some fundamentalist teaching, both at an individual and society level and thought this needed to be

explored.
- There was also concern about some worship and evangelical practice.

6. Preparing the youth worker for this work – training, support, reflection and relevance of the youth worker's own spiritual journey
   - How spirituality and spiritual development is currently taught, introduced and supported by the profession.
   - Whether the spiritual journey and experience of the worker is relevant in this work and, if so, how it is encouraged and supported.

7. The community aspect of spirituality and spiritual development
   - Spirituality is often seen as an individual occupation. Many respondents pointed out the community role and the links with social cohesion.

8. The complexity of spirituality and spiritual development and how it is delivered
   - It is not just faith organisations offering young people opportunities for spiritual development and the statutory services offering secular opportunities – it is more complex. For example, the Scouts have a spiritual value base and a strong acknowledgment of a transcendental being appropriate to a person's culture and background.

These areas, together with other more individual points, were considered and integrated into this document, which aims to give an overview of the subject. There is ample room for future research to supplement this work, in particular to capture more explicitly the voice of young people, or to document the position of the main faiths (contact details for the main faiths are available in Appendix 9 of this document).

1. The historical and faith context to the subject

1.1. Youth work from its inception has had a strong focus on values and these values have often been presented in a spiritual or religious framework. As Young says:

> *Youth work is and always has been concerned with the development of young people's values. From its beginning, commitments to 'the improvement of the **spiritual** and mental condition of young men' (YMCA 1844 Statement of Purpose, in YMCA 1987:4), the development of 'the whole personality of individual boys and girls' (HMSO 1940: para. 2) and the desire for young people to 'better equip themselves to live the life of mature, creative and responsible members of a free society' (Maud 1951:3), all expressed aspirations which were centrally concerned not with the activities in which young people participated but with the values they held and the 'kind of people' they were to become.*

> K. Young 1999(i)

1.2. This was further developed by the McNair committee as Young says:

> *In 1944 the McNair Committee commented on the need for youth workers to act as 'guides, philosophers and friends' (HMSO 1944: 103) to young people. The contention here is that youth workers should provide a steer for young people through the philosophical enquiry into the nature, significance and interrelationship of their values and beliefs, based on a relationship or true friendship – wanting for someone what one thinks good for his or her sake and not for one's own (Aristotle).*

> K. Young 1999(i)

1.3. Lord Redcliffe-Maud, Permanent Secretary of the Ministry of Education, in 1951 defined the aim of youth services as:

> *To offer individual young people in their leisure time, opportunities of various kinds, complementary to those at home, formal education and work, to discover and develop*

*their personal resources of **body in mind** and **spirit** and thus
better equip themselves to live the life of mature creative and
responsible members of the Free Society. (HMSO: 1951).*

This particularly included the spirit as a focus of youth work and this vision
of the work is continued in the Albemarle Report, as Young says:

*In 1960, the Albemarle Report declared that the youth service
was responsible for helping young people develop 'a sense
of fellowship', 'the capacity to make sound judgements' and
'mutual respect and tolerance' (HMSO 1960: 37).*

K. Young 1999 (i)

In 1998 David Blunkett writing as the Secretary of State for Education and
Employment in *The Learning Age* restated how learning develops
a spiritual side of our lives.

*As well as securing our economic future, learning has a wider
contribution. It helps make ours a civilised society, develops
a spiritual side of our lives and promotes active citizenship.
Learning enables people to play a full part in their community.
It strengthens the family, the neighbourhood and consequently
the nation.*

This developmental, community based value has been central in youth work
development and spiritual development has been a given part of this
holistic value driven approach.

*By education I mean an all-round drawing out of the best in
a child and man – body, mind and spirit.*

Mahatma Gandhi (in Follmi 2004)

1.4. Youth work has subsequently developed from this value informed approach.
In the voluntary sector youth work has built on the work of early faith
pioneers. In the statutory sector the value shaping of early work has
continued to underpin the youth work process.

1.5. The spiritual framework of youth work draws heavily on the pioneering work of early social and educational reformers from faith communities. In Victorian and pre-Victorian times the spirit of reform drew individuals into setting up social enterprises for communities. Many of these centres were concerned with young people.

1.6. A selection of examples of early 'youth workers' is found in Appendix 1 which has been copied from the www.infed.org website. Further biographies and commentaries can be viewed on the site which show that although many early informal educators in the United Kingdom were Christians other contributors to the early work included Jews, Hindus, and Muslims.

1.7. These early pioneers drew on their faiths and philosophical beliefs and often saw the principal aim of the work in terms of spiritual change.

> George Williams and the YMCA movement.
> *They set out with 'the view of uniting and directing the efforts of Christian young men for the spiritual welfare of their fellows in the various departments of commercial life' (YMCA 1857: front piece). In other words, they began by looking to the needs of people like themselves – a form of mutual aid. As the Movement grew, those involved were quick to amend rules and activities in response to the needs they identified. For example, by 1848 the object of the Association was not just 'spiritual' but also 'mental' improvement; and the concern was with young men in general.* From www.infed.org

1.8. Current work being undertaken by faith communities

Youth work in the faith sector has dramatically increased in the last ten to 15 years. This has been an increase both in the number of professionally qualified workers working in this sector, and the professionalisation of the work. For example, in Christian youth work now young people are much more likely to experience informal education delivered by trained workers which is less likely to be recreational or purely social.

In many Church of England dioceses the number of full time youth workers exceeds the number of statutory youth workers. Other faiths are also showing a keen interest in continuing to develop their work with young people. In addition, faith communities work in social action projects which focus on young people. This adds up to a significant body of work being undertaken by professional youth workers who have an explicit spiritual context to their work.

The recent NYA conferences held to look at Muslim Youth Work (December 2005 and March 2006) have produced some significant suggestions to take this work forward at a strategic and practical level. (see Khan 2006)

1.9. As this field extends and possibly expands, it is increasingly important that there is a professional confidence in how spirituality and faith 'sit' within the wider youth work agenda and practice.

For many years the lack of knowledge in the profession about religious practices has meant that there has been a reluctance to 'interfere'. Under the umbrella of equal opportunities differences were 'respected' without being really explored. In an effort to be inclusive there was a reluctance to challenge work in a faith context. This is especially true in work within the Islamic community where the appropriate sensitivity to the minority position sometimes means that dialogue is limited to safe, non-controversial areas. For a greater understanding and awareness in our communities it is essential that concepts such as spirituality, faith and religion are fully open to sensitive and informed debate.

1.10. Projects are exploring the role of faith communities and spirituality as a way of building social cohesion. Work done in an inter faith context can encourage understanding and demonstrate to young people in their communities that all the great faiths have in their teaching something termed 'the golden rule' (see Appendix 2). This entreats – in the words of each particular faith – followers of religions to be respectful of others. It is useful to view social change in terms of values and how these affect behaviour rather than simply address aggressive or protective actions which happen in the community as a result of social change. A common language based on respecting the spirituality of each other and in each other would be a powerful tool for reconciliation and positive community living. The point was widely debated and endorsed at the Muslim Youth Work conference held in December 2005. Recommendation 5: Creating a platform that enables a relationship between Muslim youth workers or youth workers who work with Muslims and the Department for Education and Skills. Muslim Youth Work Conference (page 9).

2. What is spirituality?

— a feeling. not necessarily connected to church

2.1.   There is a real problem in trying to 'define' spirituality. Some have a natural affinity with it and the word encourages them to rush towards the concept with a feeling of ownership. For others the word carries so much baggage and ill feeling they despise it and want nothing to do with it.

> *I have a friend who is a nun. She told me that when she went into a supermarket wearing her habit people had two reactions. One group would go towards her and seek her out. The other group would move to a different aisle, possibly embarrassed. I think spirituality is a lot like this.*

2.2.   In addition to the feelings invoked by the word 'spirituality' the term itself is a slippery concept. As spirituality cannot be held, tasted or heard but relates to an interior perspective it is difficult to keep it still and coherent in order to ascribe qualities to it.

2.3.   Spirituality can be intensely personal and unique so people invest a lot of energy in what it means to them. It is therefore hard to have a disinterested debate on the subject. It is essential when it is being discussed that there is mutual respect and an understanding and acceptance that spirituality can mean different things.

2.4.   On the other hand one young woman interviewed had no understanding at all of the concept and although academically able found it hard to relate at all to what this could mean in her own life.

2.5.   Research by Clapton into 'The religious experience and faith development of non-church going young people' (1993) compared church going young people with those who did not go to church. The research concluded that spiritual experiences were by no means limited to church going young people.

> *A clear picture has emerged showing the spiritual awareness of nonchurch young people. They are active in making sense of themselves, the world and the existential questions which they encounter. They are recipients of the most profound religious experiences, comparable with any reported by the church attenders. Finally, they make sense of their lives through a faith*

> which is constructed by centres of value and power, creating an
> 'ultimate environment'.
>
> T. Clapton (1993)

2.6. Spirituality is perceived by many people as being there, a part of one's humanity. Therefore a working approach that sees young people as being deficient in spirit is untenable. Responses received to the initial consultation paper were calling for the voice of young people to be amplified and powerful in this debate. The young person is seen by some as an agent for change, not merely benefiting from good 'spiritual' education but as educators and change-makers for the whole of society. Some argue that the freedom of the young from society's trappings and frameworks makes them more able to explore and promote deeper levels of understandings.

> *It is the nature of the 'new' to be carried and expressed by the*
> *young, since they are the ones who are least defended against*
> *the spirit of the time and the ones most deeply, if not always*
> *consciously embedded in it. This is why we should pay close*
> *attention to developments in youth and popular spirituality,*
> *because in and through our young we see most clearly the*
> *stirrings of the zeitgeist.*
>
> D. Tacey (2004)

2.7. Nigel Pimlott of Frontier Youth Trust has been working with the concept of spirituality and social cohesion. He writes:

> As I have the privilege of travelling up and down the country
> leading workshops on this subject, I have taken the opportunity
> of inviting workshop participants to come up with their own words
> and definitions of what is meant by 'spirituality' and 'spiritual
> development'. These are set out below for consideration as
> possible definitions.

Words associated with spirituality:

blend	non-material	breath
openness	beyond ourselves	beauty
awareness of others	divine	diverse
new/different experience	human	incomplete
exploration	fear	journey
a void	uncertainty	God/Jesus
mystical	process	personal/collect

abstract	*your God goes with you*	*wholeness*
mediums	*mystery*	*transient*
no absolutes	*the unknown*	*taboo*
hope	*inwardly turned*	*uncontrollable*
experience	*everything*	*conscious*
catharsis	*non-physical/biological*	*spirit*
peace	*reality*	*feeling/emotion*
no God	*ritual*	*enrichment*
transcendence	*communion with God*	*heart*
depth	*connection with beyond*	*a way of relating*
community	*searching for something*	*bonding with something*
new age	*indefinable*	*mantra*
arts	*quiet time/meditation*	*prayer*
connectedness	*dangerous*	*searching*
choices	*confusing*	*fulfilment*

> *The very essence of the Hindu Philosophy is that man has a spirit, and has a body and not that man is a body and may have a spirit also.*
>
> Swami Vivekananda (in Follmi 2004)

2.8. Zaehener (1997) suggests that there are four types of spirituality within and between religions:

> *Four types of spirituality:*
> - *loving union with a personal God;*
> - *a sense of oneness with the Absolute and the world;*
> - *a sense of being separate from the world; and*
> - *becoming one with one's real self.*
>
> R.C. Zaehener (1997)

2.9. Zaehener's categories for spirituality were echoed in responses to the initial consultation. One typology suggested in response to the consultation suggests two spiritualities, the first as a human search, the second as a response to a divine initiative. Another suggested typology used the terms 'formative' and 'transformative' spirituality. An extract from their forthcoming publication is below.

> *Savage, Collins-Mayo and Mayo (forthcoming) draw a distinction between 'formative spirituality' and 'transformative spirituality'. They suggest that 'formative spirituality' is a*

> broad understanding that sees spirituality as a _fundamental_
> _potential_ within the human condition, thus inherent in any
> world view. In this sense, spirituality focuses on an individual's
> sense of raised awareness of relationality (with, for example,
> self and others, and possibly God, the Universe, etc), which
> may include mystery sensing (awe, wonder, dread), meaning
> making and value sensing (delight and despair, right and
> wrong, existential meaning) (Hay with Nye, 1998). They
> call this 'formative spirituality' because it is inherent in the
> human condition. Spirituality in this sense is implicit in
> many individual actions and experiences. However, it may
> go unrecognised as such, or not of much consequence to the
> individual concerned.
>
> A narrower concept of spirituality is what is called
> 'transformative', this involves a conscious attempt to develop
> beyond formative spirituality in order to touch a deeper
> reality or transcendent realm. 'Transformative spirituality'
> involves the individual in deliberate practices (whether overtly
> 'religious' or not) which aim to foster mindfulness of the Other
> (howsoever conceived – eg God, Self, Universe) and help
> maintain a _sense of connectedness_. This spiritual mindfulness
> then has significance for the individual insofar as it _permeates_
> _daily life, guides his or her decisions and provides a continued_
> appreciation of the Other._

Savage, S., Collins-Mayo, S. and Mayo, R.
(forthcoming) _The World View of Generation Y_,
London, Church House Publishing

It was apparent in responses to the consultation that for some religious people it was impossible to take the transcendental 'other' out of spirituality and that spirituality was intricately linked with religious practice, worship and community. For many religious people the concept of a free standing spirituality apart from the transcendental 'other' was impossible.

There was a wish amongst many responding to the initial consultation for more information, knowledge and experience about how youth work is done within different faith and religious contexts. This is potentially a very useful area for future work. Appendix 9 contains details of contacts and resources of the major faith organisations.

2.10. It is important to ensure sensitivity to different faith positions and religions. Equally it is important to ensure that those who view spirituality in a different way are included. The following statement comes from the British Humanist Association.

> *... there is nothing shameful about spirituality, but ... nobody has a monopoly on it. We should not allow the term to be kidnapped for the churches and mosques and confined for the use of their clients. Wonder at the stars, love of the wilderness, enjoyment of the arts, are a human birthright. We should encourage them and practise them. We should notice the uniqueness of human personhood and the associated boundaries on conduct required by respect for that personhood.*
>
> *Such respect should extend to the buildings, poems, songs and dances of our ancestors, even when they were in the service of beliefs we cannot share. Myths have their place, as do imagination and stories, and often have an application to the here and now.*
>
> Professor Simon Blackburn, philosopher and
> vice-president of the British Humanist Association,
> writing in *The Sunday Times*, 4 February 2004

Other respondents to the consultation were keen that a good understanding of atheism and agnosticism sit alongside the understanding of major faiths. They wanted the subject to be viewed in terms of belief systems rather than faiths and include different philosophical positions as well as faith positions.

There was also an influence from 'pick and mix' beliefs where young people acquire a range of different philosophical and practice tools. This postmodern approach is sometimes called 'New Age' and ancient small society practice and wisdom, for example from the American Indians, is clustered with elements of the major faiths such as reincarnation.

There needs to be caution in the debate to honour the complexity of the subject. Even the major faiths have a range of different denominations and approaches which defy treating them with a monolithic certainty.

2.11. Another aspect of spirituality is how it is integrated in community. It is not just an individual journey but for many is embedded as part of the community experience.

Community

> *For both Jews and Christians 'Loving your neighbour as*

*yourself' is at the heart of their spirituality and Jesus' story of
the Good Samaritan shows very clearly this love of neighbour
crosses both cultural and religious divides.* EMEL – *The Muslim
Lifestyle Magazine recently had an article with this powerful
statement – 'We must reach out to our neighbours not with an
agenda of conversion but in simple acts of sincere love.'*

Bishop Roger Sainsbury: Make Space
– Youth Matters Conference 2005

Another response to the original consultation raises concerns that
'spirituality is treated as a matter of consumer choice, rather than something
that can have a transforming impact on the lives of individuals and
communities'.

The need to notice, and foster the community spirit is also cited as a factor in
community and social cohesion. Managing this dynamic positively can bring
about powerful reconciliation, understanding and trust.

2.12.   The attempt at defining spirituality is in tune with this research into the
subject. There is a divergent quality to the concept with many people seeing
different end points and goals. One group working on the concept became
quite heated when the researcher tried to 'pin' spirituality down and saw the
very act of definition as defeating the endeavour of the word.

2.13.   There were consistent images of spirituality which have emerged both
through reading and through meetings with people. These are that
spirituality:
- Is about the 'other' – either the other in terms of a God or a transcendent
being – or 'other' in terms of being different to the more mundane areas of
life.
- Is not something separate from life but flows through life almost as a
different but essential dimension.
- Is being squeezed out of people's experience because of the present
cultural expectation of achieving fulfilment through having rather than
being.
- Is connected with crises and peak experiences in one's life.
- Is something to do with relationship and connection – both with people
and in the community, and with the environment and the world.
- Is an internal sense of meaning and story – a deep understanding of 'who I
am and my place here'.
- Is not necessarily 'cosy and warm' but can be awesome and unsettling.
- Is about being 'fully human' integrating and balancing different aspects of

the self to live to one's deepest potential.
- Is about an inner 'truth' and deep self knowledge.

Be obedient to your truth   Religious Society of Friends 1994

Then what is the motive which keeps us busy in the Sufi Order,
what is our object in taking this path of initiation? Our object
in this is to become human, to find the way how to become
human, how to live a human being's life to its fullness, how to
live a life of love, harmony and beauty.

Inayat Khan (in Follmi 2004)

Truth resides in the heart of every man. And it is there that he
must seek it, in order to be guided by it so that, at the least it
will appear to him. But we do not have the right to force others
to see the Truth in our way.

Mahatma Gandhi (in Follmi 2004)

A human being is part of a whole, called by us the 'Universe,'
a part limited in time and space. He experiences himself, his
thoughts and feelings, as something separated from the rest
– a kind of optical delusion of his consciousness. This delusion
is a kind of prison for us, restricting us to our personal desires
and to affection for a few persons nearest us. Our task must
be to free ourselves from this prison by widening our circles of
compassion to embrace all living creatures and the whole of
nature in its beauty.

Albert Einstein (Quoted in H Eves
Mathematical Circles Adieu (Boston 1977)

about spirituality ...
(Some people) ... have suggested that we are talking about
an awareness that there is more to life than meets the eye,
an understanding that life is full of things that inspire awe
and wonder, a rationale that incorporates paradoxes, the
unexplained, and mysteries. Yet others have reflected upon the
sense that life is a complex journey weaved by understanding
and grappling with the issues relating to understanding
ourselves and others, the environment that we live in and the

> *un-quantifiable 'out there' subjects of god, the non material and the transcendent.*
>
> Nigel Pimlott (2005)

2.14. It could be argued that the government is trying to incorporate some of the elements of spirituality within the term 'wellbeing' which features in recent government legislation on work with children and young people. The way this term is used is much broader than simply good physical health and includes a proactive aspirational approach to life. 'Wellbeing' also seems to be inspired by a deep sense of okayness which could be linked to having a good self identity rooted in positive values – concepts many of the respondents connected with spirituality.

2.15. A point raised by many was that spirituality could not be 'domesticated'. There is a level of meaning within spirituality that is immense and it confounds restricting the concept into neat compartments. This was seen as a really positive influence in the world, spirituality has the potential of introducing creative possibilities to breathe life into sometimes sterile situations.

Dualist Framework

Many cultures use a dualist framework to construct their world and to build a common sense of meaning. Items and words have their opposites and sit with each other to bring about a balanced world, where the qualities of one of the items reflect and limit the qualities of the other.

Dark	Light		Male	Female
Sun	Moon		Hot	Cold
Body	Spirit		High	Low
Love	Hate		Rich	Poor
Sick	Well		Order	Chaos

This dualism is central to Chinese cosmology and is seen in the Yin and Yang symbols – where Yin and Yang symbolise the sun and the moon.

There are two opposing forces active in the universe. Yin exists in Yang and Yang exists in Yin. This is the changing combination of negative and positive, dark and light, cold and hot which keeps the world spinning and creates Chi – the life giving force.

Even where a culture has not got a specific mythology or ideology, dualism concepts can often be found which help frame thinking.

*It is necessary that this be the aim of our entire life. In all our
thoughts and actions, we must be conscious of the infinite.*

Rabindranath Tagore (in Follmi 2004)

*All this talk and turmoil and noise and movement is outside
the veil; inside the veil is silence and calm and peace.*

Bayezid Bistami (in Follmi 2004)

2.16. One can argue that the role of 'spirituality' in youth work is to provide a
sense of balance – to give the profession a divergent, exploratory aspect
to balance the more convergent particular outcomes and targets. This is
explored later in the paper (see section 4).

2.17. In thinking about spirituality many people cited Maslow's hierarchy of needs.
In its original form there were five 'needs' that had to be attended to 'in order'
– with the most basic needs being satisfied first. For example, if a person has
basic biological and physiological needs they will seek to satisfy these before
their need to belong. Maslow described the first four levels as deficiency
motivators and the fifth level as growth motivator. He also said that aims and
drives were focused on the next higher order needs.

Maslow's five level Hierarchy of needs model (1954)

1. Biological and Physiological needs – air, food, drink, shelter, warmth, sex,
   sleep, etc.
2. Safety needs – protection from elements, security, order, law, limits,
   stability, etc.
3. Belongingness and Love needs – work group, family, affection, relationships,
   etc.
4. Esteem needs – self-esteem, achievement, mastery, independence, status,
   dominance, prestige, managerial responsibility, etc.
5. Cognitive needs – search for knowledge, understanding, meaning etc.

It is interesting that in further developments of this model in the 1970s
another three categories have been added, namely:

6. Aesthetic needs – appreciation and search for beauty, balance, form, etc.
7. Self-actualisation needs – realising personal potential, self-fulfilment, seeking
   personal growth and peak experiences.
8. Transcendence needs – helping others to achieve self-actualisation.

People spoke of the 'fifth cognitive' need as where spirituality might 'sit' and how this is part of the education of the whole person.

From http://chiron.valdosta.edu/whuitt/col/regsys/maslow.html

Maslow's Hierarchy of Needs

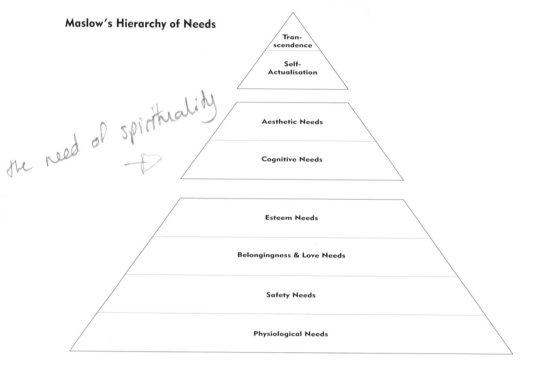

To reach cosmic understanding, it is necessary to unite our feeling with that infinite feeling that penetrates everything. In fact, for man, true progress coincides with the breadth of the base of our feelings. All our poetry, philosophy, science, art and religion serve to embrace with our understanding the spheres too vast and high.

Rabindranath Tagore (in Follmi 2004)

Maslow's model is not without criticism and many have questioned the hierarchical nature of need. A response to the initial consultation indicates the care needed when using such a model, while Batsleer expresses a concern at ...

... the use of Maslow's 'hierarchy of needs' and the linked use of 'stage' models of human development (in this case the use

of Fowler's stages to provide theoretical underpinning. For me, the idea of 'self-actualisation' as a pinnacle to a hierarchy is profoundly rooted in and conformed to individualist American culture, profoundly anti-spiritual in my understanding of spirituality and very much the subject of critique from a faith tradition that has kenosis/self-emptying at its heart. Linked to this is my knowledge of the widespread academic critique to which such 'stage' models of human development and the life course have been subject, particularly of course the critiques of Piaget and Kohlberg from feminist and other counter-hegemonic perspectives.

... I do not deny the helpfulness of models in assisting us in thinking about youth and community work as a learning process, and I do think that certainly in modern industrial societies there are particular learning moments (and crises) associated with adolescence. However, I think these models need to be thought of in a particularly sophisticated way.

Janet Batsleer – Manchester Metropolitan University

It can be argued that in spite of potential weaknesses the model has made a significant contribution to the educational debate and helped to identify different categories of need. Youth work seeks to meet a range of needs and the 'higher' needs identified in the model are evidenced as outcomes in youth work, and are especially cited in the field of outdoor education. The model can be used with care to contribute to the overall understanding of meeting basic needs and working developmentally with young people to reach the highest aims, which is very much part of youth work philosophy.

Alan Chapman on his website www.businessballs.com lists self-actualising characteristics that share many of the words and descriptions from Nigel Pimlott's list above.

relates to activities

Maslow's Self-Actualising characteristics

- keen sense of reality – aware of real situations – objective judgment, rather than subjective;
- see problems in terms of challenges and situations requiring solutions, rather than see problems as personal complaints or excuses;
- need for privacy and comfortable being alone;
- reliant on own experiences and judgment – independent – not reliant on culture and environment to form opinions and views;
- not susceptible to social pressures – non-conformist;
- democratic, fair and non-discriminating – embracing and enjoying all cultures,

races and individual styles;

- socially compassionate – possessing humanity;
- accepting others as they are and not trying to change people;
- comfortable with oneself – despite any unconventional tendencies. A few close intimate friends rather than many surface relationships;
- sense of humour directed at oneself or the human condition, rather than at the expense of others;
- spontaneous and natural – true to oneself, rather than being how others want, excited and interested in everything, even ordinary things;
- creative, inventive and original; and
- seek peak experiences that leave a lasting impression.

> *Man is setting out to satisfy needs that mean more to him than simply nourishment and clothing. He is embarking on a rediscovery of himself. The history of man is his voyage toward the unknown, in the search for the realisation of his immortal Self, of his soul.*
>
> Rabindranath Tagore (in Follmi 2004)

> *You yourself are your own obstacle – rise above yourself.*
>
> Hafiz (in Follmi 2004)

2.18. John Hull in *Youth and Policy* speaks of the quality of the spirit and argues that the spiritual is not a part to be added and is not a part of the whole but is a dimension. The spiritual dimension can no more be taken away than the third dimension can be taken away from an object.

> *The same is true of the spiritual. When we speak of the spirit of a sporting team, we refer to some quality of the behaviour and attitudes of the team as a whole, and the same is true of the 'spirit of the nation', 'the spirit of war' and so on. In such expressions we do not refer to a part of the whole, but to some energising and invigorating quality of the whole.*
>
> John Hull, *Youth and Policy*, Autumn 1999

2.19. There is also a key question about how and where spirituality 'fits' with the concept of faith and religion. John Hull in *Youth and Policy* explored the inter-relatedness of the three concepts and concluded that the concepts of faith and religion are subsumed in the concept of spirituality. He says:

> *. . . to the question of faith. Religion and spirituality are not attitudes. Spirituality . . . is the achievement of humanness, and the religions are the traditions and techniques for achieving this in relation to the transcendent Ultimate. Faith, however, has to do with subjectivity. It is the positive human response to the issues raised by spirituality.*
>
> J. Hull (1999)

2.20. It is has been virtually impossible to come up with an absolute, clean definition of spirituality which can be used in every circumstance. However, it is also apparent that 'spirituality' can have a place as a very useful shorthand to refer to this particular dimension which is an essential part of our true humanity.

3. What is spiritual development?

3.1. There are countless religious sayings and thoughts which point to spiritual growth and development:

> *Religion is a realisation, not talk, not doctrines, nor theories, however beautiful all these may be. Religion is being and becoming, not hearing and acknowledging. It is not an intellectual assent but the transformation of one's whole life.*
>
> Swami Viveknanda (in Follmi 2004)

> *When I open my heart I find truth and discretion in all things.*
>
> Mechtild of Magdeburg (www.op.org/domcentral)

> *When a man*
> *Battles with his soul,*
> *The life and the soul of the whole world enter*
> *And he is free*
>
> Rabindranath Tagore (in Follmi 2004)

> *Believe nothing that binds you to the sole authority of your masters or priests. That which you have tried yourself, which you have experienced, which you have recognised as true, and which will be beneficial to you and to others; believe that, and shape your conduct to it.*
>
> Buddha (in Follmi 2004)

3.2. The Ofsted document *Promoting and evaluating pupils' spiritual, moral, social and cultural development* identifies three elements:
Spiritual development involves:
- the development of insights, principles, beliefs, attitudes and values which guide and motivate us. For many pupils, these will have a significant religious basis;
- a developing understanding of feelings and emotions which causes us to reflect and to learn; and
- for all pupils, a developing recognition that their insights, principles, beliefs, attitudes and values should influence, inspire or guide them in life.

Ofsted then brings these together to form a working definition:

> *Spiritual development is the development of the non-material element of a human being which animates and sustains us and, depending on our point of view, either ends or continues in some form when we die. It is about the development of a sense of identity, self-worth, personal insight, meaning and purpose. It is about the development of a pupil's 'spirit'. Some people may call it the development of a pupil's 'soul'; others as the development of 'personality' or 'character'.*

In another document Ofsted has presented an outline definition of spiritual development for work in schools:

> *'Spiritual development relates to that aspect of inner life through which pupils acquire insights into their personal existence which are of enduring worth. It is characterised by reflection, the attribution of meaning to experience, valuing a non-material dimension to life and intimations of an enduring reality. 'Spiritual' is not synonymous with 'religious'; all areas of the curriculum may contribute to pupils' spiritual development.*

Ofsted Handbook for the Inspection of Schools 1994

Further definitions and information from Ofsted can be found in Appendix 8.

Following on from John Hull's theory above, spiritual development could be thought of as a process of humanisation.

> *Since the spiritual is, broadly speaking, concerned with the achievement of personhood, it may be thought of as synonymous with the process of humanisation.*
>
> *. . . becoming human is a process, the result of which is an achievement, and therefore we may speak of the process of humanisation as being our ontological vocation.* (Freire 1972).
>
> *This process may be called spiritualisation, since there is no achievement of humanness without a realisation of the human spirit.*

John Hull, *Youth and Policy*, Autumn 1999

3.3.   Nigel Pimlott, in his work around the country asking people to come up with ideas about spiritual development, got the following responses:

Spiritual Development is about:

- *a journey of discovery;*
- *a journey/point/process of discovering that there is something more than self;*
- *existing outside of faith;*
- *is it born in all of us?;*
- *a journey towards wholeness;*
- *a deepening understanding of all things not material;*
- *understanding which cannot be explained;*
- *awareness of self, others, environment and God;*
- *the long path;*
- *growth in and application of faith;*
- *growing into wholeness;*
- *the natural process that results from spiritual awareness;*
- *people growing in faith and belief;*
- *having a growing awareness of self and life and the meaning of life. It's about moving towards an integrity of personhood;*
- *if spirituality is the search for meaning and value, then spiritual development is how those searches and quests develop;*
- *spiritual development has a link with morality – knowing right and wrong. It has a link with an awareness of self and others;*
- *spirituality is being 'human' it is everlasting and in oneself and in others as you meet them; and*
- *spirituality is a process of searching within for the truth without.*

3.4.   Ofsted has also presented an outline definition of spiritual development for work in schools:

> *Spiritual development relates to that aspect of inner life through which pupils acquire insights into their personal existence which are of enduring worth. It is characterised by reflection, the attribution of meaning to experience, valuing a non-material dimension to life and intimations of an enduring reality. 'Spiritual' is not synonymous with 'religious'; all areas of the curriculum may contribute to pupils' spiritual development.*

Ofsted Handbook for the Inspection of Schools 1994

3.5.   The same difficulty in trying to find a definition is apparent in the search for an understanding of spiritual development. Nigel Pimlott of FYT writes:

> *Spiritual development is not something we can make for others. It is a journey that each individual has to take. The journey cannot be made easier by taking short cuts and everyone has their own starting point and their own final destination. It is a journey that can be shared with others and it involves challenging ourselves and the young people we work with. It involves new experiences and doesn't impose ideas and faith onto others.*
>
> N. Pimlott (2005)

3.6. Some people would also argue that spiritual development is not about achieving any particular end, rather that it is the process of increased awareness and understanding that enables a continual sense of becoming. Many religious teachings use the journey as a metaphor of continuous personal growth, rather than a description of how to get to a particular destination. This emphasis on process is very familiar to youth work method.

A journey

> *My journeys led me to one unavoidable conclusion: the Muslim paradise is not a place of arrival but a way of travelling.*
>
> Ziauddin Sardar (in Follmi 2004)

> *We want to deepen our awareness of that which is deepest in us, which responds to other people and the world around us, which gives us direction and life. Such openness and awareness has to be nurtured and encouraged. It is vital for all spiritual learning that there are opportunities for reflection, sharing, discussion and response. In a Quaker context this means we try to interpret our inward experiences in worship, listen together to discern what we must do and put our beliefs into action together.*
>
> Children and Young People's Report,
> Britain Yearly Meeting 2004, Religious Society of Friends.

3.7. Spiritual development in some faiths is seen as being through religious practice and is expressed in religious terms. This means that some people are not used to expressing spirituality as a free standing concept as it is so closely linked into the religious framework.

3.8. Different cultures and faiths have key concepts which relate to spirituality, particularly in the youth work context. Chandu Christian writing in *Youth and Policy*, Autumn 1999, writes:

> *Youth work has yet to absorb and use the multi-faith or multicultural concepts that are now available to it. For example, the concepts of Guru-Shishya as relationship, Islam as submission, the Tao as the way, Zen as a method of self-actualisation without complicated rituals, the Shabad (Word) as a revelation – these and many other concepts are now part of our multi-cultural legacy. Youth work can apply them for both personal and spiritual development of young people as well as to create a tolerant and understanding society.*

C. Christian (1999)

3.9. There are some theologians who have produced theories of faith development. Most notable in the Christian tradition are Fowler and Westerhof – see appendix 3 for further information. The Quakers have used these theories and combined them with the work of John Lee, a former Diocesan Youth Officer for the Church of England, to come up with a matrix for spiritual development (see appendix 3). The ecumenical training resource for youth workers, Spectrum, has also developed a spiritual quest model, see appendix 4.

3.10. The idea of spiritual development is one which is linked to the idea of 'becoming' and can be viewed either as a free standing concept or as a concept that is deeply embedded and integrated within a religious framework.

If spirituality is a dimension of experience as is argued above, then spiritual development has the potential of occurring from all experience. Obviously some experiences will be more fruitful than others in enabling a young person to deepen their understanding and awareness.

As in other development models learning is enhanced when the young person 'notices' or registers the experience. This indicates two ways in which the youth worker can aid the spiritual development process. The first is by giving opportunities and experiences which are spiritually rich, the second is to facilitate the young person's reflection on their spiritual learning.

4. What is the role of spirituality and spiritual development in youth work?

> *The purpose of youth work is to ensure that young people have a good death. Good youth work process gives young people tools to reach their full potential so that when they die, in old age, they can look back on a life of achievement and feel deep contentment.*
>
> Maxine Green at the first NYA/DfES spirituality meeting 2004

In this section several key threads which contribute to the debate are explored. In the conclusion there are some broad observations relating to these key threads.

> *We need to restore the place of spirituality in the public as well as the private world, relating it to truth as well as to personal experience. It should be understood as the essential source of character development for a society based on sacrificial love.*
>
> Youth A Part, 1996

4.1. The responses to the consultation paper resoundingly supported work in the area of spirituality and spiritual development and stressed how important it was for youth work.

There is a real need for the informal work on spirituality in the youth service to work in parallel with the 'formal' work in schools and colleges. For this to be most useful there needs to be an understanding of content and approach in the schools curriculum so that the youth work process can be complementary.

4.2. Historical continuity

Many times when youth work has been called to describe itself the value based nature of the profession has been reiterated. The values of equality, empowerment, education and participation emerge from a philosophy of the profession which is about the whole nature of the young person. Even where reports have not been explicit about this there is an implicit understanding that youth work is holistic. It is not just about increasing skills, changing behaviour or imparting knowledge, it is about development of the whole of the young person. In the early shaping of the profession this was spelled out as the development of body, mind and spirit. At different times in the history of youth work one or another element has been in the ascendancy. For example, some early youth work was very much focused on the spirit. Later with the rise of outdoor education as a youth work tool the development of the body was seen to be the key. In the last five or ten years the emphasis has moved to accrediting specific skills and in some cases the wider aims of youth work and informal education have been taken over by the need to achieve particular targets.

The youth work profession is able to put a strong case forward that achievements are stronger and more sustained if they are gained from an integrated whole person approach. However, where funding streams encourage this targeted work it becomes even more important that the holistic approach is upheld.

As spirituality and spiritual development are part of the whole of youth work, maintaining an understanding of how and where these occur in youth work is one way of ensuring the holistic approach continues.

4.3.   National Occupational Standards

Spiritual development is part of National Occupational Standards (see Appendix 5). It could be argued that many of the standards which are looking at overall growth and development of young people include an element relating to spirituality. The key purpose of youth work as outlined in the National Occupational Standards gives an indication of the whole person approach:

> *The key purpose of youth work is to work with young people to facilitate their personal, social and educational development, and enable them to gain a voice, influence and place in society in a period of their transition from dependence to independence.*

While spiritual development is not mentioned specifically in the Key Purpose it is an integral part of personal and social development. As the overall purpose is divided into sections the role of spirituality can be traced within the standards. For example, Section A states: 'Build relationships with young people which enable them to explore and make sense of their experiences and plan and take action.' For young people who have an awareness of their spiritual life this would necessarily be part of their exploration, their experience and would feature in how they make future plans. Some would argue that this spiritual aspect is also there for young people without a particular spiritual framework and that it features as a spiritual dimension to their lives and experience even if it is not named and specifically acknowledged.

The National Occupational Standards have a unit with a particular focus on spirituality. Section B is to 'Facilitate young people's learning and their personal and social development'. Unit B.2.2. has the specific focus to:

Assist young people in the exploration and development of their spiritual self:

> *This is about encouraging young people to see themselves in a wider setting of relationships with others and with the environment around them. It is about enabling young people to have a sense of and a value to their life journey.*

The unit describes knowledge, behaviour and values which constitute an approach to spirituality and spiritual development. It describes how young people should be encouraged to understand and know their own spiritual framework, how they can recognise and respect others' religion, faith and spirituality and how they can use an awareness of their spiritual selves 'to explore their feelings at times of great joy or pain in their lives.'

The inclusion of a unit which focuses on the 'spiritual self' is to be welcomed, both for professionals working in a faith setting and for those working in a secular context.

This unit provides a challenge for the profession in how this standard can be met. The youth worker working in a faith context is challenged to give a broad approach, whilst the youth worker working in a secular post is challenged to find ways of exploring this dimension of young people's experience.

> *That soul which does not attain to the degree of purity corresponding with the light and vocation it has received from God can never be wholly content and at peace. St John of the Cross (in Ruth 1985)*

4.4.   Young people's developmental stage

Young people are at a stage where they are integrating different aspects of themselves. It is a stage where they endeavour to make sense of the world and construct their personal philosophy and sense of meaning. This is a time when many young people wrestle with existential questions and try and make sense of their own place in the world and their purpose in being alive. Trudi Newton has integrated Pam Levin's theory of 'Cycles of development' with Jean Ilsley-Clarke's theory to produce a developmental model (see Appendix 6). The model has six developmental stages with the sixth stage from 13 to 18 years being the 'integration' stage.

Stage	Tasks of young person	Needs, strokes	Stages in Change
Integration 13 to 18-years	Separate Be independent Be responsible Have own needs Have own values Integrate sexuality	Understand Encourage Accept Support Discuss Celebrate	Application and Integration

Newton indicates firstly, the tasks of the young person from each stage and secondly, what they need from others to complete these tasks successfully to enable development and growth. She says that in the integration stage the young person will call upon the ways they have developed in the past and integrate them as they build up their new identity. For example, the teenager will withdraw, explore, try new ways of doing things. They will learn at this time to apply new skills appropriately and understand the context in which they do things.

This integration task is one where the young person revisits and reshapes the skills acquired in their earlier years into a framework which is connected to the community framework they find themselves in. By understanding themselves they are then able to separate, become independent, responsible and start to shape their adult identity. Their spirituality is a key component in this integration, for young people with a faith or with other beliefs. John Hull's idea of 'humanisation' couldn't be more appropriate a concept for this stage.

The youth worker role is also made explicit using this model – that is to understand, encourage, accept, support, discuss and celebrate with the young person.

4.5. The role of youth worker

> *The time of adolescence is particularly turbulent for a young*
> *person. Who am I? becomes a particularly demanding question.*
> *In their struggle for an answer the youth worker or animateur*
> *has a particular role to play. Formal education may enable*
> *a young person to be more in harmony with the external*
> *world (to wit Bowen and Bloom), and as a consequence*
> *with their own individual self. Youth work enables a young*
> *person to be more in harmony with his or her own self and*
> *as a consequence with the rest of the world. Both formal and*
> *informal education thus have a part to play in enabling young*
> *people to find their 'real' selves.*
>
> Chandu Christian (1999)

Christian in his article about spirituality in the context of multi-cultural youth work looks at the complementary role of formal and informal education. With formal education helping the young person become more in harmony with the external world and informal education helping the young person to be in harmony with his or her self. The features of this harmony with self could be broadly summed up in Maslow's self actualisation characteristics. As already stated these characteristics correlate closely with people's perceptions of spirituality and spiritual development. Youth workers, therefore have this potentially powerful role in helping young people know themselves, their 'real selves', and develop a sense of meaning and identity within their lives.

4.6. The organisation Oasis in its response to the consultation lists areas which it views as important:-

Attention should be given to activities that promote spiritual awareness and development:
a.   It is important to generate space for young people to ask questions in the area of spirituality. This is often limited because there are few presentations of what is actually going on in this area.
b.   Youth projects can present information in the area of spirituality as one option among others, as part of an ongoing informal education programme that might normally include subjects with less obvious spiritual dimensions (eg sexual health). One example given was presentation of materials on the Jewish memorial of the Holocaust.
c.   Youth workers and volunteers need training as to how to run such activities.
d.   Youth workers and volunteers need exposure to alternative religions

and spiritualities, for example
- visits to religious centres (mosques, mandirs, etc); and
- assignments that require students to interview young people of different faith traditions about particular spiritual issues.

West Sussex Youth Service Curriculum has Spiritual Development as one of its content areas:

> *In our view good practice is embodied in youth work which:*
> - *Is sensitive to young people's customs, and needs for worship.*
> - *Helps young people face difficult (and sometimes unanswerable) questions.*
> - *Facilitates the understanding of the beliefs of others.*
> - *Offers opportunities for young people to think beyond the immediate.*
> - *Includes an exploration of the spiritual dimension of individual experiences.*
> - *Encourages awareness in young people that they are part of the human family and can reach out to others.*

4.7. Many respondents to the consultation thought that the training and support for youth workers in this field was vital.

The 1996 Conference arranged by the National Association for Outdoor Education and hosted by Westhill College concluded that to bring a more holistic approach to youth work the following was required:
- more staff trained in facilitating transpersonal development;
- a new language that conveyed spirituality in everyday terms; and
- a tool box of activities and resources which facilitators could use.

> *People who work in most educational support services have a profound lack of personal experience and confidence in working with issues of spirituality. Effectively, the main need in terms of policy and practice is for training of youth workers in how to work with young people in a spiritual or transpersonal way.*

> University for Spirit Forum – response to consultancy paper

How to address this in professional training is an issue which elicits different opinions. Many youth workers are currently being trained in courses which combine youth work with theology. This enables more time to be spent on the theological and arguably addresses spirituality in more depth. These courses are more likely to be Christian in conception although Muslim students do attend these courses in small numbers. There are also specific plans to develop Muslim youth work courses, potentially alongside Christian youth work programmes to confer professional youth work qualifications. However, there are other voices in the debate which challenge this approach.

> I don't think that running separate faith based BA level courses is helpful – if there is sufficient space given to spirituality in all courses a multi approach environment would provide an excellent training ground for those from all backgrounds.

> Carole Pugh, University of Durham
> – response to consultancy paper

In both approaches most respondents to the consultation thought that it was a necessary focus within professional development which could be summed up as follows:

Professional youth work training should take a holistic approach, addressing:
a.   Issues of personal spirituality as part of professional development.
b.   The spiritual dimension of the overall ethos of particular youth work projects.
c.   How to ensure that spirituality figures significantly in the youth work curriculum.

4.8.   The 'subversive'/enriching role of spirituality in youth work

In an earlier section dualism was explored with the concepts of Yin and Yang. There has been debate in youth work over the last five to ten years about the effect of increased targeting of the work. The profession is being encouraged to look more and more at specific outcomes for young people. A lot of creative thought has been brought to bear by youth work staff and thinkers about how the existing 'products' of youth work can be recognised and accredited. There is widespread understanding of the advantages to young people when they can recognise distance travelled and outcomes achieved.

However, another effect of increasing targeting is that youth work practice can change so that its success is measured principally in targets achieved. This can have a detrimental effect on the holistic, relationship based approach which is embedded in the values of the profession. By having something like 'spirituality' in the curriculum and practice there is a whole area which is much harder to pin down and constrain. The divergent nature of 'spiritual development' means that outcomes are much wider and individual. The outcomes are nearly all in the changes of value and meaning for the young person and these are much harder to quantify than a skill or piece of knowledge which can more easily be tested or monitored. Spirituality and spiritual development are by their nature 'free' subjects, and exploration of these areas potentially puts young people in touch with profound thinkers and social reformers.

Where a lot of work with young people is geared towards education, employment and training, spiritual development is primarily about being a full human being. Spirituality as an area of the curriculum has the potential for exploring values at a deeper more profound level which results in the full education of the young person. It can also inform the other areas of education as Christian outlined in his article (see above). Ideally, formal and informal education are complementary, both are needed for full and healthy development of the young person. In short, the inclusion of spirituality and spiritual development in the youth work agenda enriches the profession and the offer to young people.

4.9. Preparing young people to be canny about spiritual matters

The quest for continually more satisfying and exciting experiences can lead to a disengagement from reality and can further alienate young people from those churches that do not provide constant positive experiences.
Nigel Pimlott (2005)

There is a concern in some areas (especially those who are concerned about recruitment into new religious movements) about the vulnerability of young people to spiritual argument and persuasion. Young people who have not had any structured contact with their own spirituality may have a range of experiences which are incoherently yet powerfully held. At a time when young people want to break away and become independent there is a great temptation to adopt a religious or spiritual framework in which their own experiences may find a home. If on the other hand young people have been encouraged to understand their own spirituality and develop a spiritual framework they have a language and facility in matters of spirituality and are potentially more canny and able to question other faith or spiritual approaches. Some young people will develop this framework within a religious context, and for these young people the challenge is understanding how others approach religion and spirituality and to recognise, appreciate and hopefully celebrate difference (see *A Sense of Respect* by Green and Heaney). For those young people in a secular context the challenge is to find ways of facilitating the development of their spiritual framework, understanding others and becoming astute or canny about spiritual dynamics. This is an integral part of the empowerment aspect of youth work. It also is key in developing understanding which contributes to building positive communities and community cohesion and developing an understanding of equality.

> *When 'I' and 'You' are absent, I've no idea if this is a mosque, synagogue, church or temple.*
>
> Mahmud Sahbistari (in Follmi 2004)

4.10   Negative spirituality

Several people responding to the consultation were anxious that the negative effects of work in this field were highlighted. There were concerns raised about fundamentalist teaching which encouraged loyalty and a false sense of trust and discouraged questioning and thought. Techniques to convert can be at odds with the empowerment agenda of youth work and can also be abusive to young people. Negative religious teaching can affect both whole communities and individuals.

> *I have personal issues with churches that brainwash young people when they are vulnerable, as a local evangelist church has done with my eldest son (18). I accept that it is part of his journey and trust that he is intelligent enough to move beyond their blinkered vision eventually, but in the meantime they have actually taught him that I, his own mother, am evil because I do not work in their way, and if he ever talks to me it is only to try desperately to save my soul by converting me.*

Response to the consultation

The profession needs to be more comfortable around religion with youth workers able to question and challenge each other for good practice to emerge and be sustained.

4.11.   Broad observations on the above threads

The above threads give points of connection between spirituality and the youth work profession. There is a historical continuity, spirituality is part of the standards of the profession, spiritual development is a feature of adolescent maturation and it 'fits' with the holistic approach of the youth worker. Also it can be seen how spirituality as part of the youth work agenda brings a divergent quality to the curriculum and has the potential of 'lifting' the work and bringing it alive. Finally, there is a need to spiritually equip young people so that they can manage the world with discernment and spiritual skills. The presence of spirituality in the profession could be seen as the 'breath' of the profession, the animation that Christian refers to in his article that enables the holistic development of young people.

5. Key areas for the field to address arising from this debate

5.1. How to provide opportunities for young people to explore their spirituality

> *A youth worker took a group of ten boys, aged 14 and 15, for a walk in Derbyshire. He knew the country well and planned the route with great care. He took the view that few young people actually enjoy walking for its own sake and therefore the journey had to be interspersed with a number of activities and incidents.*
>
> *The group was shown the route on a map, and someone was elected to find the route for the first part of the way. After a mile or two the group went through an old railway tunnel stopping at the centre point where it was not possible to see the light from either end. There was a good deal of clowning around in the total darkness. A little later the group stopped by a dew point and the response to the question 'How long do we stay here?' was 'five minutes or until the first one falls in'. Nobody did ...*
>
> *After lunch the youth worker took a geological hammer from his rucksack and chipped away at some pieces of rock. Asked what he was doing he responded, 'go away, I'm busy'. Within ten minutes everyone was hunting for fossils and talking about them . . . The afternoon stop was taken by a stream and the youth worker encouraged the group to take off their boots and socks and paddle. No one had done this in a mountain stream before. The final stage of the walk included a sunset and a view – and the route had been chosen with this in mind.*
>
> *Effective Youth Work* (HMI, 1987)

In the example above, which now sounds a bit dated, the youth worker is using a series of pre-planned activities to enable the young people to experience different things. The activities are paced, are different and 'touch' different parts of the young men's experience. Being in total dark, experiencing the cold of a mountain stream, pondering on the age of rocks and fossilised creatures and viewing a sunset all have the potential to evoke awe and wonder. All offer the chance of understanding the self in relation to different parts of the world. If these young people lived in a city and had been taken out of a city environment the changes and learning could have been immense.

The open ended divergent offer encourages a space where a sense of meaning and understanding of self can take place. Many people when asked about spiritual experiences talk of wonder and awe and many have found this through nature.

Similarly, social justice issues present questions and queries in young people's minds which have to be processed – what is happening here and what is my role or relationship with it?

Nigel Pimlott speaks of how spirituality and spiritual development are part of the work of the Frontier Youth Trust. There is more information about spiritual work in a secular setting at Appendix 7.

> *I am also not advocating a necessarily complex approach. We can do some very simple things that provide really positive experiences. For example, if we are talking about 'the light' then why not use things like candles in a dark setting to illustrate the point in a hands on way. If we are talking about 'sowing seeds', then why not sow some and watch them grow. If we are talking about 'serving' then why not visit an old people's home and engage in some conversation and games. I know this is really basic to some, but it is easy to forget the need to be experiential and practical in our approach.*
>
> *If the experiences can have a sense of mystery about them I consider this all the better in helping engage young people. Promoting 'mystery' means that the experience will help trigger responses that develop further exploration and enquiry. This should ensure that it is not just experiences that we are offering to young people, but stepping stones to learning and discovery.*
>
> Nigel Pimlott (2005)

A popular misconception about spiritual and faith development is that it encourages dependency – the following quotes from Indian spirituality challenge this perception.

> *It is not a question of belief.*
> *Stop believing in that which is;*
> *This is the first stage. Dare to be rational.*
> *Dare to follow reason where it may take you.*
>
> Swami Vivekanda (in Follmi 2004)

To grow is to go beyond what you are today.
Stand up as yourself. Do not imitate.
Do not pretend to have achieved your goal,
and do not try to cut corners.
Just try to grow.

Swami Prajnanpad (in Follmi 2004)

Never under any circumstances ask 'how'.
When you use the word 'how' you really want someone to tell
you what to do, some guide, some system, someone to lead you
by the hand so that you lose your freedom, your capacity to
observe, your own activities, your own thoughts your own way
of life.

Krishamurti (in Follmi 2004)

The outward freedom that we shall attain will only be in exact
proportion to the inward freedom to which we may have grown
at any given moment.

Mahatma Gandhi (in Follmi 2004)

A real challenge for the sector is to understand how we can work with spirituality in a faith or secular context and to share this learning across the profession.

5.2.   Spirituality and spiritual development does not have to be the focus of work with young people. It can be an important outcome of broader work. The arts and outdoor education have been important vehicles for young people to explore their spirituality. Bishop Roger Sainsbury spoke of spirituality in music:

This year I spent time in a music workshop in Portishead Youth
Centre where there is a golden disc of the group Portishead.
Two of their songs 'Money talks and leaves us hypnotised' and
'Western Eyes' expressed a relevant spirituality for today's world.

Bishop Roger Sainsbury: Make Space
– Youth Matters Conference 2005

Other arts such as drama, visual arts, photography and media are all used by youth workers to encourage young people to be reflective and gain understanding of themselves and others.

Outdoor education also gives young people enormous opportunities to see the world and themselves with new vision.

> *... I am aware of the value of the outdoors as a setting*
> *conducive to spiritual development.*
> *It continues, even in today's more secular society, to be a*
> *setting distinctively conducive to spiritual development,*
> *whether faith based or otherwise.*

> Dr K B Everard, Chair of the Development Training
> Employers Group Institute for Outdoor Learning,
> in response to the consultation

5.3. Role of faith communities and other organisations in developing spirituality

For many religions or faith traditions there is a keenness to provide teaching, background and context about spiritual practice. This helps give young people a faith resource which they can use to frame their own spiritual experience and understanding. In some cases it can also discourage the young person from coming to their own understanding of their spiritual self. Some faiths do not view spirituality in an individual way – it is seen as an integral part of community life and there is not the option of an individual rejecting faith as it means the rejection of the community.

There is an interesting juxtaposition of where the community belonging meets the concept of individual freedom and rights. This paper is not going to be able to 'solve' this interesting and rich dynamic. It is, however, important that there is an active dialogue in the profession which throws light on the tensions that can be there for some young people. It is by understanding these that youth workers can help young people to enjoy belonging and developing their spirituality with their community, enjoy the benefits of individual options and choices and come to a positive understanding of what it best means for them.

There are also organisations which are not faith related but work within a framework of beliefs and values (eg The British Humanist Society). These too have a vital role in educating and supporting young people in their development.

5.4. What spiritual development means in a secular/statutory setting

The human soul travels from the law to love,
from discipline to freedom,
from the moral plane to the spiritual plane.

Rabindranath Tagore (in Follmi 2004)

Many youth workers who are employed in a statutory or secular context can feel uncomfortable about the notion of spiritual development. The National Occupational Standard requires workers to understand their spiritual self, know the difference between spirituality, faith and religion and be able to facilitate a range of activities to enable young people to relate to the world in a spiritual way (from NOS Unit B2 Knowledge specification see Appendix 5). If a youth worker has not had the experience or opportunity to look at this aspect of themselves it can be a daunting prospect.

Linking Maslow's characteristics of self actualisation with the wider understanding of spirituality gives a range of outcomes for which the broad youth work process is well equipped. It can be argued that spirituality is based on broad values which are coherent with those that underpin youth work method. If the work is based on values such as informal education, equality of opportunity, empowerment and participation and if the process of engagement is voluntary and through a relationship there is a coherence with the respect that is outlined in the 'Golden Rule' (see Appendix 2). This gives a starting point for the dialogue and work regarding spiritual development.

It is also important that this element of youth work is developed – by sharing good practice, through basic training and through academic and policy discussion. One reason why there is apprehension about exploring spirituality and developing spiritual frameworks is a lack of basic knowledge.

There can also be apprehension around working with different faiths and workers can be inhibited by their lack of knowledge and not wishing to offend. A lot of work undertaken recently looking at social cohesion indicates that communities grow closer when they have an understanding of each others' faiths and religious practices. As social cohesion and community development is part of the broad aim of youth work making spirituality a more explicit element in the curriculum could bring about positive consequences for the community.

The recent NYA publication *A Sense of Respect* by Maxine Green and Carmel Heaney offers a resource which youth workers can use to encourage dialogue across different faith and philosophical perspectives.

5.5.   Spirituality and spiritual development in other organisations

The area of spirituality, faith and religion in youth work is complex and it is important that in trying to grasp the scope of the subject that these complexities are not lost within broad assumptions. Assumptions that are in the field include:

*   Statutory work is secular, voluntary work is more likely to be faith based and spiritual.
*   Spirituality in youth work is likely to be provided by religious organisations.
*   Work done by religious organisations is with aims to convert.

These sort of assumptions detract from important youth work undertaken by many organisations. For example, The Scouts who work with 28 million young people internationally and approximately half a million in the United Kingdom have a formal expectation relating to 'Duty to God'. This was expressed originally as the Scout Promise in 1908:

> On my honour I promise that –
> 1. I will do my duty to God and the King.
> 2. I will do my best to help others whatever it costs me.
> 3. I know the scout law, and will obey it.
>
> The current version of the UK Scout Promise is in terms which refer, as the young person may find most appropriate to 'God' (most faiths including Christians, Hindus, Jews, Muslims and Sikhs): 'my Dharma' (Hindu alternative, Buddhists) or, 'Allah' (Orthodox Muslims): and 'duty to God' is defined as 'Adherence to spiritual principles, loyalty to the religion that expressed them and an acceptance of the duties resulting therefrom':
>
> While the aim of Scouting is to promote the development of young people in achieving their full physical, intellectual, social and spiritual potentials, as individuals, as responsible citizens and as members of their local, national and international communities.

Response to the consultation from
John Bevan, Scout Association

5.6. Spiritual process and learning outcomes

There is a huge reluctance among some people to think of spiritual outcomes. Some people think that spirituality is hard enough to define so that trying to pin down spiritual outcomes is a step too far. However, many faiths, especially in their monastic orders, will have measures of spiritual stages. For example, in Theravada Buddhism there is a well documented scheme of meditative development through meditative states which are called Jhanas. For each Jhana there are clearly formulated descriptions of the phenomena which are associated with the stage. For example, the third Jhana is associated with the experience of waves of joy which is called piti. In Christian mysticism people have also documented stages with accompanying states and phenomena. For example, Teresa of Avila documents each stage using the metaphor of an interior castle. These measures of spiritual development are used in the context of a culture and tradition of spiritual wisdom. The context is also developed in a framework of non-attachment where there is not the notion of evolutionary, linear progress and gathering and acquiring skills.

Therefore, if we choose to document spiritual development through outcomes we need to ensure a culture and context of wisdom which is apart from the progressive, acquiring model of education. The current government stresses that education is for individuals to acquire skills and knowledge for their personal use, for future work and in order to become citizens. This means that there is a potential conflict with the 'non-progress' world view which accompanies much spiritual learning.

Having said all of this the level of spiritual development explored here is much deeper than most people will choose to follow. But it does highlight the dilemma of providing defined spiritual outcomes within a current educational framework of skill and knowledge acquisition. Indeed, it could be argued that because spirituality does operate in this other world view, or framework, engaging with spirituality can offer a real and profound opportunity for young people to experience the world in a different way.

5.7. Social justice, social action and spirituality

The notion of participation in its widest sense is a keystone for youth work. Having a voice and challenging discrimination and disadvantage has always been part of the youth work agenda. For many people social justice emerges directly from their faith and their spiritual framework. Many faiths have strong expectations on how to treat others and have strong views on inequality and injustice. If the youth worker encourages young people to reflect on their spiritual values they can also support them to express them in the community and support any social action which is based on these values. Much community cohesion work and reconciliation work encourages young people to reflect on their religious and other values and check these out with their actions. The reference earlier in the paper to the 'Golden Rule' (Appendix 2) shows that respect and tolerance are found in the teachings of all faiths.

Some religions have tenets that encourage positive behaviour in the community and the corporate use of these to develop a corporate spirituality can help a group of young people to have a good community spirit.

Some denominations have strong expectations about how members should behave and values they should hold. These may concern charity, work with disadvantaged people, social justice and active campaigning. For example, to become a Quaker there is an expectation that you will follow the peace testimony. There is also a strong tradition of campaigning and non violent protest.

Satisfy the hunger of others
And your hunger will be appeased
All by itself.

His Holiness M.R. Bawa Muhaiyaddeen (in Griffiths, 1994)

Hear from the heart wordless mysteries!
Understand what cannot be understood!
In man's stone-dark heart there burns a fire
That burns all veils to their root and foundation.
When the veils are burned away, the heart will understand
completely ...
Ancient Love will unfold ever-fresh forms
In the heart of the Spirit, in the core of the heart.

Rumi (in Griffiths 1994)

We must speak the silent cry of those who today suffer from
want, hunger, disease, powerlessness and lack of freedom.

Chief Rabbi Jonathan Sacks

6. Conclusions

It is hard to conclude an exploration into the subject of spirituality and spiritual development in youth work. This is partly because of the divergent, holistic nature of the subject which resists categorisation and tidy solutions. It is also because individual youth workers have developed the spiritual dimension of their work bringing their own individual spirit to this work and to try and conflate these into a discipline feels in some way disrespectful. Having said this if the profession uses these sentiments to 'back off' the subject of spirituality it will be in real danger of getting lost and being relegated behind other more easily quantifiable targets and aims.

The consultation process and this subsequent paper from The National Youth Agency and the Department for Education and Skills have aimed to raise key areas for the field. However, this is only the beginning and it is hoped that this will be a useful tool to continue a debate, which needs to be respectful and mindful of others' interests and faith/belief positions but also needs to be undertaken in a spirit of rigour and vigour.

Appendix 1   Contribution of people with faith to informal education and youth work

Lily Montagu (1873–1963), Pioneer of youth work. One of the founders of the National Organisation of Girls Clubs (now Youth Clubs UK) and a key figure in the development of Jewish youth work.

Lily Montagu (1873–1963), with **Maud Stanley**, is one of the key figures in the development of girls' clubs and work with young women. Her contribution was fourfold. First, she was a committed worker with young people. As a young woman (19) in 1893 she set up the club with her cousin in two rooms at 71 Dean Street W1 (the club was later to move to 8 Frith Street, then 8 Dean Street). The character of her work can be gauged from her own comments: 'A club worker must enter on her career in the learning spirit. She must not attempt to foist her standards on the girls among whom she intends to work. She must study their standards, and exchange her point of view with theirs' (Montagu 1954: 24). She placed an emphasis on sharing the government of the club with members; and on educational endeavours. The latter included discussions around various moral questions and citizenship. There was also a flourishing drama group. Second, Montagu placed a particular emphasis on campaigning and working for the improvement of young women's working conditions – and this she carried into the political arena via organisations such as the Women's Industrial Council. Third, she was central to the formation and development of the National Organisation of Girls' Clubs. Last, she has left several important additions to the literature of youth work – including the account of her work at West Central (Montagu 1904; 1954). www.infed.org

Rabindranath Tagore (1861–1941), Asia's first Nobel Laureate, was born into a prominent Calcutta family known for its socio-religious and cultural innovations during the 19th Bengal Renaissance.

I was brought up in an atmosphere of aspiration, aspiration for the expansion of the human spirit. We in our home sought freedom of power in our language, freedom of imagination in our literature, freedom of soul in our religious creeds and that of mind in our social environment. Such an opportunity has given me confidence in the power of education which is one with life and which can give us real freedom, the highest that is claimed for man, his freedom of moral communion in the human world . . . I try to assert in my words and works that education has its only meaning and object in freedom – freedom from ignorance about the laws of the universe, and freedom from passion and prejudice in our communication with the human world. In my institution I have attempted to create an atmosphere of naturalness in our relationship with strangers, and the spirit of hospitality which is the first virtue in men that made civilization possible.

I invited thinkers and scholars from foreign lands to let our boys know how easy it is to realise our common fellowship, when we deal with those who are great, and that it is the puny who with their petty vanities set up barriers between man and man. (Rabindranath Tagore 1929: 73–74)

We have come to this world to accept it, not merely to know it. We may become powerful by knowledge, but we attain fullness by sympathy. The highest education is that which does not merely give us information but makes our life in harmony with all existence. But we find that this education of sympathy is not only systematically ignored in schools, but it is severely repressed. From our very childhood habits are formed and knowledge is imparted in such a manner that our life is weaned away from nature and our mind and the world are set in opposition from the beginning of our days. Thus the greatest of educations for which we came prepared is neglected, and we are made to lose our world to find a bagful of information instead. We rob the child of his earth to teach him geography, of language to teach him grammar. His hunger is for the Epic, but he is supplied with chronicles of facts and dates ... Child-nature protests against such calamity with all its power of suffering, subdued at last into silence by punishment. (Rabindranath Tagore, Personality, 1917: 116-17)   www.infed.org

Hannah More (1745–1833). The significance of Hannah and Martha More's activities with regard to Sunday schooling lay in the pedagogy they developed; the range of activities they became involved in; and the extent to which publicity concerning their activities encouraged others to develop initiatives. Hannah and Martha More attempted to make school sessions entertaining and varied. We can see this from the outline of her methods published in *Hints on how to run a Sunday School* (and reported in Roberts 1834). Programmes had to be planned and suited to the level of the students; there needed to be variety; and classes had to be as entertaining as possible (she advised using singing when energy and attention was waning). She also argued that it was possible to get the best out of children if their affections 'were engaged by kindness'. Furthermore, she made the case that terror did not pay (Young and Ashton 1956: 239). However, she still believed it was a 'fundamental error to consider children as innocent beings' rather than as beings of 'a corrupt nature and evil dispositions' (More 1799: 44, quoted by Thompson 1968: 441).

Hannah More could be said to have summed up the prevailing Evangelical attitude when she wrote: 'Action is the life of virtue, and the world is the theatre of action' (More 1808, quoted by Bebbington 1989: 12).

Other women like **Ellen Ranyard** and **Maude Stanley** were to follow in her footsteps – but just what are we to make of Hannah More's contribution to the development of different forms of informal education – especially youth work?

First, it can be argued that she worked with young people – but significantly they were only one part of the clientele she was concerned with. Hannah More was also interested in the education of children and adults – and both her writing and her activities in Sunday schooling reflect this. To this extent, she can be understood as a theorist and practitioner of lifelong education and learning. Second, she and her sister worked with people on the basis of choice. While there were all sorts of incentives to children and young people, for example, to attend Sunday schooling, Hannah More recognised that they could not be compelled to take part.

Third, relative to the schooling activities of her day, Sunday schools associated with the More sisters had a more informal air, and used a range of methods. There was more of a concern with creating the right atmosphere and relationship for learning. Besides classes there were other community and welfare interventions plus some concern with social life (and this was to be a feature of later Sunday school developments). This said, the work that Hannah More was engaged in was some distance from what we later came to know as youth work. In particular, hers is an individualistic orientation. There is little recognition here of the significance of association, group and club – and her understanding of education is very firmly conditioned by her desire to convert.

George Williams and the YMCA. During June and early July 1844 a series of discussions took place in rooms above Hitchcock and Roger's drapers shop in St Paul's Churchyard. **George Williams, Christopher Smith, Edward Valentine, John Symons,** and the eight, nine or ten other young men involved, discussed setting up what quickly became known as The Young Men's Christian Association. (The debate over the number of young men involved in the original meeting where the Association was formed is reviewed by Binfield 1973: 120–121. The discussion concerning title can be found in Shedd et al 1955: 23). They set out with 'the view of uniting and directing the efforts of Christian young men for the spiritual welfare of their fellows in the various departments of commercial life' (YMCA 1857: frontpiece). In other words, they began by looking to the needs of people like themselves – a form of mutual aid. As the Movement grew, those involved were quick to amend rules and activities in response to the needs they identified. For example, by 1848 the object of the Association was not just 'spiritual' but also 'mental' improvement; and the concern was with young men in general.

Appendix 2 The Golden Rule

Bahá'í faith
Lay not on any soul a load which ye would not wish to be laid upon you, and desire not for anyone the things ye would not desire for yourselves. This is my best counsel unto you, did ye but observe it Bah'u'allah: Gleanings, 128

Buddhism
Just as a mother would protect her only child with her life, even so let one cultivate a boundless love towards all beings. Khuddaka Patha: Metta Sutta

Christianity
Do unto others as you would have them do to you. Luke 6:31

Hinduism
This is the sum of duty; do naught to others if done to thee would cause thee pain. Mahabharata 5.1517

Islam
No one of you is a believer until he desires for his brother that which he desires for himself. An-Nawawi's Forty Hadith 13

Jainism
I forgive all beings, may all beings forgive me, I have friendship towards all, malice towards none. Pratikraman Sutra 35:49

Judaism
What is hateful to you, do not do to your fellow man. Talmud; Shabbat 31a

Sikhism
No one is my enemy, and no one is a stranger. I get along with everyone. Sri Guru Granth Sahip p.1299

Zorastrianism
That nature only is good when it shall not do unto another whatever is not good for its own self. Dadistan-I-Dinik 94.5

From *Connect*
The Inter Faith Network for the United kingdom

Appendix 3 Faith/spiritual development theories

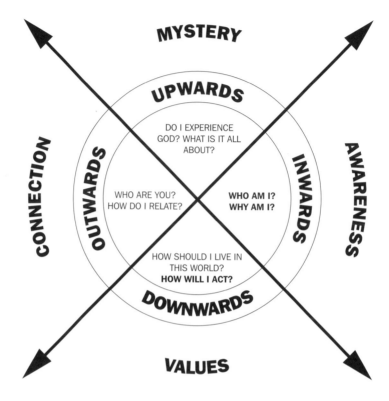

The Religious Society of Friends (Quakers) has integrated faith/spiritual development theories from Fowler, Westerhof and Lee.

One of the best known of these schemes is that offered by John H Westerhoff III, the popular writer on Christian education. He speaks of 'four distinctive styles of faith', acknowledging his indebtedness to Fowler's work. At one point Westerhoff writes of the styles of faith as being like the annual rings of a tree. A tree with one ring 'is a complete and whole tree' and a tree with three rings 'is not a better tree but only an expanded tree' (WOCHF 90). Like a tree we expand from one style of faith to another slowly and gradually, always bearing within ourselves our earlier styles of faith.

Fowler also recognises that adults are still 6-years-old 'inside', but his emphasis lies more with the results of that faith and the contents of the earlier faith stage. These are the things that tend to be carried over and that need to be reworked as we adopt a new faith form. Each Fowler stage marks the rise of new capacities and strengths that are added to and 'recontextualise' earlier patterns without 'negating or supplanting them' (SF 274). Westerhoff's position sounds similar.

> *As we expand in faith we do not leave one style of faith behind to acquire a new style but, on the contrary, each new style is added to the previous ones.*
>
> (WOCHF 90f)

But Westerhoff draws slightly different implications from his view. For him the re-adoption of earlier styles of faith is a simple matter. It can occur at any time if the needs of an earlier style of faith (for example, for experiences of trust or of belonging) cease to be met. Progression only occurs when these needs are satisfied; and the subject then moves on to satisfy other, developing concerns.

Westerhoff's tree-trunk analogy may be pictured thus:

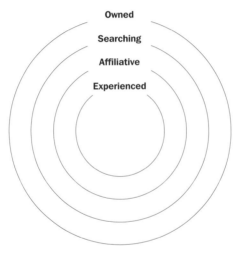

Owned

Searching

Affiliative

Experienced

The four styles of faith that Westerhoff postulated are as follows. They can be fairly readily correlated with Fowler's stages

1. **Experienced Faith** is the active and responding faith of the pre-school years and early childhood, which is experienced in the child's relationships to others. (Presumably this would be equivalent to Fowler's Stages 0 and 1.)

2. **Affiliative Faith** is the 'belonging faith' of later childhood/early adolescence, dominated by the religious affections, significant others and their stories, and the authority of a community. (This may cover Fowler's Stages 2 and 3.)

3. **Searching Faith** is common in late adolescence/early adulthood and comprises (i) doubt and/or critical judgment (as the 'religion of the heart'), (ii) experimentation with alternative understandings and ways, and (iii) the need for commitment to persons and causes – the last two elements sometimes giving the impression of fickleness as various ideologies are experimented with in rapid succession. (Is this the transition between 3 and 4?)

4. **Owned Faith** integrates the previous stages into a witnessing faith stance, a new personal faith-identity that is expressed in both word and deed. (This is equivalent to Fowler's Stage 4.)

Unlike Fowler, Westerhoff describes faith development movement itself as 'conversion' (cf WOCHF 98).

In a more recent book, Westerhoff admits that he now prefers to speak of three 'pathways' or 'trails' to God, which may be travelled 'at any time, in any order', adding that we may 'return to any trail at will'. Here he combines the first two styles of faith into a description of the 'slow, easy path' of the nurturing Affiliative – Experiencing Way, which he contrasts with the more demanding, rocky road of the Illuminative – Reflective Way where 'there is no marked trail' for the increasingly independent questers (this is clearly the time for 'searching faith'). The third path, which combines the first two, is the Unitive – Integrating Way.

> *On this complex path the community encourages persons*
> *to move back and forth between the two previous ways and*
> *thereby create a new way. (p45)*

Interdependent persons on this path combine intellectual and intuitive ways of knowing, become aware of pluralism, and are 'open to other possibilities' and the value of the other paths. This account thus sounds like a development of Westerhoff's 'owned faith' into something very reminiscent of Fowler's Stage 5.

The strength of Westerhoff's view probably lies in the vividness of his metaphors (for example, of the treetrunk) and the way in which he relates faith development to the processes of Christian learning and discipleship. Westerhoff's contribution may be viewed to a large extent as a popular reinterpretation of Fowler's research.

Steps in Faith Development/Spiritual Growth (based on a model by J.H. Westerhoff)

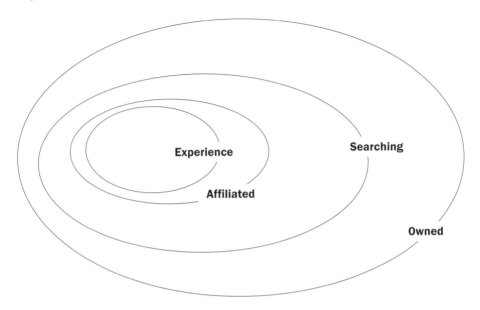

Quaker framework

Westerhoff 'Growth Rings'			
John Lee's four directions	EXPERIENCED	AFFILIATED Being alongside	SEEKING
INWARDS Who am I? Why am I? **Awareness**	THE WAY I AM TREATED	THAT OF GOD IN ME	TRYING/TESTING TESTIMONIES
OUTWARDS Who are you? How do I relate to others? **Connection**	TRAVELLING TOGETHER – FELLOW PILGRIMS	THAT OF GOD IN YOU	. . . WITH OTHERS
DOWNWARDS How should I live in this world? How will I act? **Values**	THE COMMUNITY OF FRIENDS	. . . OUR QUAKER RESPONSIBILITIES	QUAKER TESTIMONIES AND VALUES IN OUTSIDE WORLD
UPWARDS Do I experience God? What is it all about? **Values**	THAT OF GOD	SHARING THESE MOMENTS	MAKING MEETING FOR WORSHIP MY OWN

Religious Society of Friends. Children and Young People's Report Britain Yearly Meeting 2004.

Appendix 4   Spectrum model

Spectrum model of spiritual development

Spectrum NCEC 1996

Appendix 5 National Occupational Standards

UNIT: B.2   **Enable young people to develop their awareness of their self-identity and being**

ELEMENT: B.2.2   **Assist young people in the exploration and development of their spiritual self**

This is about: exploring the difference between spirituality, religion and faith, encouraging young people to see themselves in a wider setting of relationships with others and the environment around them. It is about enabling young people to have a sense of and value their life journey.

Performance Criteria You will need to know:	Knowledge Specification You will need to know:
a. Recognise and understand your own spiritual self, and its influence on the way in which you work with young people. b. Work with young people to agree the difference between spirituality, religion and faith. c. Work with young people to examine the range of aspects of spirituality. d. Share your own sense of spirituality where appropriate, without imposing your beliefs on young people. e. Develop activities to assist young people to notice aspects that they find spiritual in the world around them. f. Assist young people to explore their feelings at times of great joy or pain in their lives. g. Encourage young people to reflect on where they are in their life journey. h. Assist young people to start to develop their own spiritual framework. i. Encourage young people to develop understanding and respect for people with spiritual and religious beliefs that are different to their own.	1. Why it is important to be clear about your own spiritual self. 2. Ways in which your own beliefs and views may influence the way you work with others. 3. Why it is important to encourage young people to reflect on their spiritual relationship to the world and life, as well as their physical, emotional and rational relationship. 4. The difference between spirituality, religion and faith. 5. A range of views on spirituality, spiritual and religious beliefs. 6. A range of activities and experiences through which young people can relate to the world in a spiritual way. 7. A range of techniques to enable young people to identify the nature of their own spiritual journey through life, and reflect on where they are on that journey. 8. How to work with young people to encourage respect for and understanding of beliefs they do not share.

Notes on this element:

I. aspects of spirituality: wonder, acceptance, compassion, integrity, commitment and curiosity.

II. spiritual framework: the set of spiritual values, beliefs and practices by which they live.

Appendix 6   Newton's developmental stages

Cycles of Development

Cycles of Development

Stages		Tasks of child	Needs, strokes	Stages in Change
1 **Being** 0–6 months		learn to get needs met; learn to trust; bond emotionally; accept care, touch.	love, care, touch; consistency; you belong here; think for baby.	Immobilisation
2 **Doing** 6–18 months		explore and experience; develop senses, initiative; learn to get help; form secure attachment.	safety, encouragement, variety, protection, support; don't interrupt; OK to be active, quiet.	Denial
3 **Thinking** 1.5–3 years		learn to think, test reality; solve problems, express feelings; begin to separate; give up being centre.	encourage thinking; give reasons, how-tos; accept feelings; set limits.	Frustration
4 **Identity** 3–6 years		assert separate identity; acquire info about self, place in family; test power; social behaviour; separate fantasy/reality.	both sexes are OK; give information; answer questions; stroke OK behaviour; get own support.	Acceptance
5 **Skills** 6–12 years		learn skills; make mistakes; listen; reason; rules and structure in and out of family; values; disagree; test ideas; cooperate	lots of strokes! Be reliable, clear; offer tools; set rules; allow consequences; challenge behaviour.	Development
6 **Integration** 13–18 years		separate; be independent, responsible; have own needs, values; integrate sexuality.	understand, encourage, accept, support, discuss, celebrate.	Application
7 **Recycling**				Completion

FSPS: CYC_DEV1 @ Trudi Newton 1993 based on Pam Levin, *Cycles of Development*, and Jean Illesley-Clarke, *Growing Up Again*.

Appendix 7   Frontier Youth Trust's ways of working with spirituality (taken from *Inspire Too* pages 32-36)

How to look at spirituality in a secular setting with young people

Wow! – take young people to the top of a mountain, take them to see the sun rise, the tide come in, the waves crash against the rocks. More often than not they will be 'wowed' by the experience. They will not just see the image that fills their eyes, but will engage with the bigger mystery of nature and how it all came about. You could try a canoe trip, a camp fire in the wilds or a night spent wandering in a dark forest. All will stimulate the bigger questions of where we came from. (Be careful as there are health and safety issues associated with many of these activities.)

Silence and Pondering
Our world is very busy and many young people will never (and I mean, never) have experienced total silence. Sitting in a field, relaxing in a hall or community building with just a few candles burning can create an environment where young people can consider their inner state, experience a sense of calm and for some, overcome their fear of silence.

Joy and Sorrow
Joy happens when things in life can be celebrated. These might be formal occasions such as birthdays and anniversaries or more informal occasions such as celebrating a bright and hot sunny day, a goal scored by your favourite team or a satisfying meal. All these occasions can be used to help young people reflect on the spiritual side of life. We can look back at times past, or look forward to times to come. Emotions and inner feelings can be explored and appraised.

There are times when young people can be very unhappy. They might have suffered a loss, an illness or be feeling depressed. The British are less good at expressing these feelings than people from other backgrounds. Perhaps we could learn from others and do some art, some reflective writing, or carry out some act of remembrance to explore these issues in a practical way.

Creativity
Making things enables many people to express their spirituality in ways that they could never do if they just used words. Things like sculpture (clay, wax, plasticine) playing a musical instrument, painting and graffiti all enable the deep side of us to express itself.

If expressing creativity is new to you, give it a go and listen to the heart that is behind the creation. If you don't like actually creating yourself, choose something that someone else has created (a painting, a sculpture) and pose the same questions – what is the artist saying?

What spiritually is going on?

The Big Questions in Life

Whether we have a faith or not, researchers would tend to confirm that we always ask the same basic questions about life: 'who am I?', 'where have I come from?' and 'where am I going?'. The questions might be phrased differently, but the central motivation of the questions resides in these three overarching questions.

Even atheists and humanists must have asked themselves these questions in order to come to their own 'faith' conclusions! My experience would indicate that these remain questions young people are very interested in.

Other 'Big' Questions

In answering the big three questions above we will inevitably consider our place in society and the wider world. It is during these discussions and interactions with young people that we can consider a number of other issues that focus on issues that have a strong spiritual dynamic:

> ***Personal discipline and morality*** – what is my code of behaviour and how have I come to live by it and believe it?

> ***Tolerance and Respect*** – where do I fit in the world and take my place alongside people who are different to me?

> ***Understanding the world*** – why is there so much suffering in the world and how can I do my bit for the planet (or should I do my bit for the planet?)

Frontier Youth Trust p 21

Appendix 8   Further definitions of spirituality

Ofsted's 1994 comments complemented views which were set out in a document from the National Curriculum Council (NCC) – *Spiritual and Moral Development – A Discussion Paper*. This usefully defined different aspects of spiritual development:

'Beliefs – the development of personal beliefs including religious beliefs; an appreciation that people have individual and shared beliefs on which they base their lives; a developing understanding of how beliefs contribute to personal identity.
A sense of awe, wonder and mystery – being inspired by the natural world, mystery or human achievement.
Experiencing feelings of transcendence – feelings which may give rise to belief in the existence of a divine being or the belief that one's inner resources provide the ability to rise above everyday experiences.
Search for meaning and purpose – asking 'why me?' at times of hardship and suffering; reflecting on the origins and purpose of life; responding to challenging experiences of life such as beauty, suffering and death.
Self-knowledge – an awareness of oneself in terms of thoughts, feelings, emotions, responsibilities and experiences; a growing understanding and acceptance of individual identity; an ability to build up relationships with others.
Relationships – recognising and valuing the worth of each individual; developing a sense of community; the ability to build up relationships with others.
Creativity – expressing innermost thoughts and feelings through, for example, art, music, literature and crafts; exercising the imagination, inspiration, intuition and insight.
Feelings and emotions – the sense of being moved by beauty or kindness; hurt by injustice or aggression; a growing awareness of when it is important to control emotions and feelings, and how to learn to use such feelings as a source of growth.'

It also added that:
'Spiritual development is an important element of a child's education and fundamental to other areas of learning. Without curiosity, without the inclination to question, and without the exercise of imagination, insight and intuition, young people would lack the motivation to learn, and their intellectual development would be impaired. Deprived of self-understanding and potentially the ability to understand others, they may experience difficulty in co-existing with neighbours and colleagues to the detriment of their social development. Were they not able to be moved by feelings of awe and wonder at the beauty of the world we live in, or the power of artists, musicians and writers to manipulate space, sound and language, they would live in an inner spiritual and cultural desert'.

Three years later, the School Curriculum and Assessment Authority (SCAA) produced a report which defined spirituality as some or all of:

'the essence of being human, involving the ability to surpass the boundaries of the physical and material;
an inner life, insight and vision;
an inclination to believe in ideals and possibilities that transcend our experience of the world

a response to God, the 'other' or the 'ultimate';
a propensity to foster human attributes such as love, faithfulness and goodness, that could not be classed as physical;
the inner world of creativity and imagination;
the quest for meaning in life, for truth and ultimate values; and
the sense of identity and self-worth which enables us to value others.'

The paper also recognised the important link between spiritual development and learning:

'A spiritual sense can be seen as a prerequisite for learning since it is the human spirit that motivates us to reach beyond ourselves and existing knowledge to search for explanations of existence. The human spirit engaged in a search for truth could be a definition of education, challenging young people to explore and develop their own spirituality and helping them in their own search for truth.'
Education for Adult Life: The Spiritual and Moral Development of Young People. London, SCAA, 1996.

Pupils who are developing spiritually are likely to be developing some or all of the following characteristics:

- a set of values, principles and beliefs, which may or may not be religious, which inform their perspective on life and their patterns of behaviour;
- an awareness and understanding of their own and others' beliefs;
- a respect for themselves and for others;
- a sense of empathy with others, concern and compassion;
- an increasing ability to reflect and learn from this reflection;
- an ability to show courage and persistence in defence of their aims, values, principles and beliefs;
- a readiness to challenge all that would constrain the human spirit: for example, poverty of aspiration, lack of self-confidence and belief, moral neutrality or indifference, force, fanaticism, aggression, greed, injustice, narrowness of vision, self-interest, sexism, racism and other forms of discrimination;
- an appreciation of the intangible – for example, beauty, truth, love, goodness, order – as well as for mystery, paradox and ambiguity;
- a respect for insight as well as for knowledge and reason;
- an expressive and/or creative impulse;
- an ability to think in terms of the 'whole' – for example, concepts such as harmony, interdependence, scale, perspective; and
- an understanding of feelings and emotions, and their likely impact.

Schools that are encouraging pupils' spiritual development are, therefore, likely to be:

- giving pupils the opportunity to explore values and beliefs, including religious beliefs, and the way in which they affect people's lives;
- where pupils already have religious beliefs, supporting and developing these beliefs in ways which are personal and relevant to them;

- encouraging pupils to explore and develop what animates themselves and others encouraging pupils to reflect and learn from reflection;
- giving pupils the opportunity to understand human feelings and emotions, the way they affect people and how an understanding of them can be helpful;
- developing a climate or ethos within which all pupils can grow and flourish, respect others and be respected; and
- accommodating difference and respecting the integrity of individuals.

And promoting teaching styles which:

- value pupils' questions and give them space for their own thoughts, ideas and concerns;
- enable pupils to make connections between aspects of their learning; and
- encourage pupils to relate their learning to a wider frame of reference – for example, asking 'why?', 'how?' and 'where?' as well as 'what?', monitoring, in simple, pragmatic ways, the success of what is provided.

U Thant, former Secretary General of the United Nations

> *Spirituality is a state of connectedness to life.*
> *It is an experience of being, belonging and caring.*
>
> *It is sensitivity and compassion, joy and hope.*
> *It is harmony between the innermost life and the outer life,*
> *or the life of the world and the life of the universe.*
> *It is the supreme comprehension of life in time and space,*
> *the tuning of the inner person with the great mysteries*
> *and secrets that are around us.*
>
> *It is the belief in the goodness of life*
> *and the possibility for each human person*
> *to contribute goodness to it.*
>
> *It is the belief in life as part of the eternal stream of time,*
> *that each of us came from somewhere and is destined to*
> *somewhere, that*
> *without such belief there could be no prayer,*
> *no meditation, no peace, and no happiness.*

Appendix 9   Contacts and Resources

Organisations

Inter faith organisations

The Inter Faith Network for the United Kingdom
The Inter Faith Network for the UK works to build good relations between the communities of all the major faiths in Britain: Bahá'í; Buddhist; Christian; Hindu; Jain; Jewish; Muslim; Sikh; and Zoroastrian.

Address: 8A Lower Grosvenor Place, London SW1W 0EN.
Telephone: 020 7931 7766.
Fax: 020 7931 7722.
E-mail: ifnet@interfaith.org.uk
Website: www.interfaith.org.uk

MultiFaithNet
MultiFaithNet is a gateway to information on world religions: Bahá'í; Buddhism; Christianity; Hinduism; Islam; Jainism; Judaism; Sikhism; Zoroastrianism and Inter faith. There is a short introduction to each religion and links to other resources.

Address: Multi-Faith Centre, University of Derby, Kedleston Road, Derbyshire Street, Derby DE22 1GB.
Website: www.multifaithnet.org

Maimonides Foundation
Links Jewish and Muslim faiths.

Address: Nour House, 6 Hill Street, London W1J 5NF.
Telephone: 020 7518 8282.
E-mail: info@maimonides–foundation.org
Website: www.maimonides–foundation.org.uk

Council of Christians and Jews
To promote good relations between Christian and Jewish communities.

Telephone: 020 7820 0090.
E-mail: cjrelations@ccj.org.uk
Website: www.ccj.org.uk

Minorities of Europe
A Pan-European inter-minority network which seeks to support and assist

the cooperation, solidarity and exchange between different minority communities and young people in Europe.

Address: Legacy House, 29 Walsgrave Road, Coventry CV2 4HE.
Telephone: 024 7622 5764.
E-mail: admin@moe-online.com
Website: www.moe-online.com

Faith organisations

National Spiritual Assembly of the Bahá'í
The National Spiritual Assembly is the elected governing body of members of the Bahá'í faith in the UK.

Address: 27 Rutland Gate, London SW7 1PD.
Telephone: 020 7584 2566.
Fax: 020 7584 9402.
E-mail: nsa@bahai.org.uk
Website: www.bahai.org.uk

Network of Buddhist Organisations
Founded in 1993 to promote fellowship and dialogue between Buddhist organisations, to facilitate cooperation in matters of common interest and to work in harmony with Buddhist and likeminded organisations around the world.

Address: 6 Tyne Road, Bishopston, Bristol BS7 8EE.
Helpline: 0845 345 8978.
E-mail: secretary@nbo.org.uk
Website: www.nbo.org.uk

Churches Together in Britain and Ireland
There are many different Christian churches and denominations, but all have the same basic calling: to worship God, to share the good news about Jesus Christ and to work for the good of all people. When they work together they are acting as Churches Together.

Address: 3rd Floor, Bastille Court, 2 Paris Garden, London SE1 8ND.
Telephone: 020 7654 7254.
E-mail: info@ctbi.org.uk
Website: www.ctbi.org.uk

Hindu Council
Founded in 1994 and links a wide range of Hindu organisations.

Address: 126–128 Uxbridge Road, London W13 8QS.
Telephone: 020 8566 5656.
E-mail: info@hinducounciluk.org
Website: www.hinducounciluk.org

Jain Samaj Europe
Address: 20 James Close. London NW11 9QX.
Telephone: 020 8455 5573.
E-mail: natubhaishah@aol.com

The Board of Deputies of British Jews
For over 240 years the Board of Deputies has protected, supported and defended the interests, rights and customs of Jews in the United Kingdom and promoted the development of the Jewish community in Britain.
Address: 6 Bloomsbury Square, London WC1A 2LP.
Telephone: 020 7543 5400.
E-mail: info@bod.org.uk
Website: www.bod.org.uk

Muslim Council of Britain
The Muslim Council of Britain aims to promote cooperation, consensus and unity on Muslim affairs in the UK, to encourage and strengthen all existing efforts being made for the benefit of the Muslim community, to work for a more enlightened appreciation of Islam and Muslims in wider society, to establish a position for the Muslim community within British society that is fair and based on due rights, to work for the eradication of disadvantages and forms of discrimination faced by Muslims, to foster better community relations and work for the good of society as a whole.
Address: Boardman House, 64 Broadway, Stratford, London E15 1NT.
Telephone: 020 8432 0585/6.
Fax: 020 8432 0587.
E-mail: admin@mcb.org.uk
Website: www.mcb.org.uk

Network of Sikh Organisations
National body promoting Sikhism in the UK. The NSO aims to establish unity and cooperation between all Sikh organisations in the UK, whether or not they are affiliated to the NSO. Run with the active participation of more than 70 leading Gurdwaras and other Sikh organisations.
Address: Suite 405, Highland House, 165 The Broadway, Wimbledon, London SW19 1NE.
Telephone: 020 8540 4148.
Website: www.nsouk.co.uk

Zoroastrian Trust Funds of Europe
Address: Zoroastrian Centre, 440 Alexandra Avenue, Harrow, Middlesex HA2 9TL.

Telephone: 020 8866 0765.
E-mail: secretary@ztfe.com
Website: www.ztfe.com

Humanist and secular organisations

Humanism

Humanism is the belief that people can live good lives without religious
or superstitious beliefs. Humanists make sense of the world using reason,
experience and shared human values.

Address: British Humanist Association, 1 Gower Street, London WC1E 6HD.
Telephone: 020 7079 3580.
Website: www.humanism.org.uk

Secularism
The National Secular Society is the leading British group speaking out for the
rights of atheists, agnostics and all other non-believers. Its aim is to fight
religious prejudice and privilege. It affirms that no-one should be
disadvantaged because they do not subscribe to a religious faith.

Address: National Secular Society, 25 Red Lion Square, London WC1R 4RL.
Telephone: 020 7404 3126.
Website: www.secularism.org.uk

Websites

Many of the organisations above have helpful websites. Other useful
websites include:

BBC religions website
The BBC religions website contains useful information including an A–Z of
religious beliefs, message boards, articles about faith in society today and
statistics about religion around the world.

Website: www.bbc.co.uk/religion/religions

Faith Communities Unit at the Home Office – www.homeoffice.gov.uk
www.belief.net

Save the Children Diversity and Dialogue project: www.savethechildren.
org.uk/diversityanddialogue

Books

Religion and spirituality, Moss, Bernard, Russell House Publishing, 2005, ISBN 1903855578. £13.95.
This book uses a celebration of diversity and the need to treat others with dignity and respect as a starting point to discuss increasing recognition in various fields of people's religious and spiritual needs and explains why the issues should be taken seriously.

Faith, citizenship and community cohesion – executive summary, Foster, Michelle, Save the Children, 2004, free.
Summary of the research into issues of faith schools, citizenship and community cohesion, examining the views of young people in three faith schools on their understanding of other faiths and cultures and the value they place on contact with other faiths and cultures. It looks at what the young people perceived to be the bridges and the barriers and how they think faith schools might promote cultural contact and integration.

Religion in England and Wales: findings from the 2001 Home Office Citizenship Survey, O'Beirne, Maria, Home Office Research Directorate, 2004. ISBN 1844731804. Free.
Survey intended to map the relevance of religion in the lives of people in England and Wales. Using data from over 15,000 interviews it looks at religious affiliation, self identity and religion, religious discrimination, and religion as a driver of social and civic participation and attitudes. Website: www.homeoffice.gov.uk/rds

Local Inter Faith Activity in the UK: A Survey, The Inter Faith Network for the United Kingdom, 2003. ISBN 190290611X. £8.95
Survey of local inter faith initiatives around the UK. Information on all forms of inter faith activity with a particular focus on inter faith and multi faith groups, councils, forums and networks. It also includes information on how local authorities are responding to faith and inter faith issues. Available from The Inter Faith Network for the UK, 8A Lower Grosvenor Place, London SW1W 0EN.

Good practice guide in ecumenical youth work, Madden, Pat, Churches Together in Britain, 2002. ISBN 1874285204. £4.00.
Report which brings together a picture of innovative work with young people which can be achieved when churches work together. Key issues are also identified. Available from Churches Together in Britain, 3rd Floor, Bastille Court, 2 Paris Garden, London SE1 8ND.

Inter Faith Organisations in the UK: a directory, The Inter Faith Network for the United Kingdom, second edition 2005. ISBN 1902906179. £4.95.
Gives contact details for over 200 organisations working to promote good inter faith relations at UK, national, regional and local level. Available from The Inter Faith Network for the UK, 8A Lower Grosvenor Place, London SW1W 0EN.

The Local Inter Faith Guide, The Inter Faith Network for the United Kingdom, 1999. Second edition due out later in 2005 (includes information on dietary issues).

Connect: Different Faiths, Shared Values, The Inter Faith Network for the United Kingdom with The National Youth Agency and TimeBank, 2004.

Religions in the UK: directory 2001–03, Multi-Faith Centre at the University of Derby in association with The Inter Faith Network for the United Kingdom, 2001. ISBN 0901437964. £25.00.
Designed to assist and encourage the development of inter faith contacts and dialogue in the UK.

Multi-Faith Britain: an experiment in worship, Hart, David A., O Books, 2002. ISBN 1903816084. £8.99.
Collection of essays which present different views and understandings around the prospect of a multi-faith Britain.

Issues: Religions and Beliefs in Britain, Craig Donnellan (ed), Independence, 2005. ISBN 1861683022. Collection of articles looking at religious diversity and tolerance in Britain. Available from Independence. Website: www.independence.co.uk

List of Faith Community Body Contacts

Bahá'í

The National Spiritual Assembly of Bahá'ís
27 Rutland Gate
London
SW7 1PD

Tel: 020 7584 2566
E-mail: nsa@bahai.org.uk
www.bahai.org.uk

Buddhist

The Network of Buddhist Organisations (UK)
c/o 6 Tyne Road
Bishopstone
Bristol
BS7 8EE

Tel: 0845 345 8978
E-mail: secretary@nbo.org.uk
www.nbo.org.uk

The Buddhist Society
58 Eccleston Square
London
SW1V 1PH

Tel: 020 7834 5858
E-mail: info@thebuddhistsociety.org
www.thebuddhistsociety.org

Hindu

Hindu Council (UK)
126–128 Uxbridge Road
London
W13 8QS

Tel: 020 8566 5658
E-mail: office@hinducounciluk.org
www.hinducounciluk.org

Hindu Forum of Britain
Unit 3, Vascroft Estate
861 Coronation Road
Park Royal
London
NW10 7PT

Tel: 020 8965 0671
E-mail: info@hinduforum.org
www.hinduforum.org

Jain

Jain Samaj Europe
c/o 20 James Close
London
NW11 9QX

Tel: 020 8455 5573
E-mail: natubhaishah@aol.com

Institute of Jainology
Unit 18, Silicon Business Centre
26–28 Wadsworth Road

Greenford
Middlesex
UB6 7JZ

Tel: 020 8997 2300
E-mail: info@jainology.org
www.jainology.org

Jewish

Board of Deputies of British Jews
6 Bloomsbury Square
London
WC1A 2LP

Tel: 020 7543 5400
E-mail: info@bod.org.uk
www.bod.org.uk

United Synagogue
Adler House
735 High Road
N12 0US

Tel: 020 8343 8989
E-mail: info@unitedsynagogue.org.uk
www.unitedsynagogue.org.uk

Reform Synagogues of Great Britain
The Sternberg Centre for Judaism
The Manor House
80 East End Road
London
N3 2SY

Tel: 020 8349 4731
E-mail: admin@reformjudaism.org.uk
www.reformjudaism.org.uk

Liberal Judaism
The Montagu Centre
21 Maple Street
London
W1T 4BE

Tel: 020 7580 1663
E-mail: montagu@liberaljudaism.org
www.liberaljudaism.org

Muslim

The Muslim Council of Britain
Boardman House
64 Broadway
Stratford
London
E15 1NT

Tel: 020 8432 0585/6
E-mail: admin@mcb.org.uk
www.mcb.org.uk

British Muslim Forum
Eaton Hall
Retford, Nottinghamshire
DN22 0PR

Tel: 01777 706441
E-mail: info@britishmuslimforum.org
www.britishmuslimforum.org

Imams and Mosques Council
20–22 Creffield Road
London
W5 3RP

Tel: 020 8992 6636
E-mail: msraza@muslimcollege.ac.uk
www.muslimcollege.ac.uk

The Islamic Cultural Centre Regent's Park
146 Park Road
London
NW8 7RG

Tel: 020 7724 3363
E-mail: info@iccuk.org
www.iccuk.org

World Ahlul-Bayt Islamic League
19A Chelmsford Square
London
NW10 3AP

Tel: 020 8459 8475
E-mail: wabil@wabil.com
www.wabil.com

Al-Khoei Foundation
Stone Hall,
Chevening Road
London
NW6 6TN

Tel: 020 7372 4049
E-mail: yousuf@al-khoei.demon.co.uk

Sikh

Network of Sikh Organisations (UK)
43 Dorset Road
Merton Park
London
SW19 3EZ

Tel: 020 8540 4148
E-mail: sikhmessenger@aol.com
www.nsouk.co.uk

Zoroastrian

Zoroastrian Trust Funds of Europe
The Zoroastrian Centre
440 Alexandra Avenue
Harrow
Middlesex HA2 9TL

Tel: 020 8866 0765
E-mail: secretary@ztfe.com
www.ztfe.com

Appendix 10 Respondees to consultation

List of people responding to the consultation paper – the views they represent are not necessarily those of their organisations

Respondent	From
David O'Malley	SBD
Janet Batsleer	Head of Youth and Community Work MMU
Ingrid Cranfield	Endeavour Training
Mark Waghorn	Scout Association
Paul Oginsky	Western Spirit
Jeremy Thomson	Oasis Youth Work and Ministry course
Jonathan Melville-Thomas	Kingston & Wimbledon YMCA
Jonathan Cruickshank	
Mark Hobbs-Shoulder	Wiltshire Youth Service
Cheryl Hunt	Exeter ESRC Seminar series
Douglas Stephenson	Brahma Kumaris World Spiritual University
Sharon Court	Portsmouth City Council Youth Service
Ben Holloway	Oxford Youth Works
Dave Pegg	Exeter
Pete White	Youth and Children's Worker, St Giles Church Northampton
Peter Hart	Youth and Children's Worker, Stranton Church, Hartlepool
Bob Mayo	
Donald MacDonald	

Respondent	From
Roger Orgill	University for Spirit Forum & Stoneleigh Group
John Bevan	
Carole Pugh	Durham University
Dawn Bishop	Council for Environmental Education
Mike Fordham	Young@now
Chris Devereaux	W. A. Consultants
Neal Terry	
D. J. Rackham	
Chandu Christian	
Marilyn Mason	British Humanist Association
Reverend E. Quildan	
Dave Horton and Centre of Youth Ministry Students	
Matt Wilson	The Message Manchester
Nick Lear	
Michael Smith	Southwell House Youth Project London
Tim Sudworth	Youth Adviser, Guildford
Maggie Startup and Ofsted team	Ofsted
Julia Woodman	Radiance Solutions
Paul Levy and Simon Best	Rowntree Fellows 2005
Claire Haddon	Rotherham Young People's Services
Graham Hill	West Sussex County Council Youth Service

Respondent	From
National and Diocesan Youth Officers from the Church of England	
John Emery	Hull Youth Service
Three mixed youth workers/student groups Durham University	
Fidelma Meehan	Bahá'ís of Swindon
Dr K B Everard	Chair of the Development Training Employers Group
Institute for Outdoor Learning	

Appendix 11

Letter from Bishop Roger Sainsbury, Chair of The NYA
(from the original consultation document)

Dear Colleague

I would like to invite you to be part of a consultation on the subject of Spirituality and Spiritual Development in Youth Work.

This document is a consultation paper to collect thoughts and ideas from the youth work field to help form a collective understanding about spirituality and spiritual development in youth work.

The consultation paper was commissioned by the Department for Education and Skills from The National Youth Agency. The commissioning of this paper follows several meetings which included people in the field to extend our thinking on spirituality and spiritual development in the changing context of young people's lives. The paper was drafted by Maxine Green.

Spiritual development is one of the key aims of modern youth work and is part of the National Occupational Standards. Hence it is important to know what the concept now represents and how the youth work profession should respond to this area of work. This paper has been written with a view to capturing the key areas where spirituality and spiritual development connect and are part of youth work.

Views are being sought from the field during Spring and Summer 2005 and feedback from this consultation will inform a paper to be written later in 2005. The aim of the final paper will be to clarify the present place of spirituality and spiritual development in youth work and to inform professional reflection, policy and practice.

Feedback, comments and views are requested in two areas. Firstly, with a view to the whole document, to check any significant omissions and inaccuracies and any areas of the subject which need further explanation or clarification. Questions to prompt responses follow this letter and are included in the response section at the end of the document. Secondly, on the specific issues which are raised in the debate. Questions on these issues are distributed through the text with a proforma for responses at the end of the document.

Yours sincerely

+ Roger Sny

Questions relating to the whole report

1. To what extent do you find the overall paper convincing? Where are its strengths and weak points?

2. Are there any serious omissions from the paper, in terms of important literature or arguments, ideas and positions that are unjustly neglected?

3. Are there any elements in the paper that could be further strengthened? Do you have additional evidence to support these? Are there significant nuances, angles or implications which have been neglected?

4. In the light of your reactions to the earlier questions and to the body of the paper, what further questions need to be asked to stimulate this debate?

5. At this stage, what do you think are the main implications for future research, and for policy and practice?

6. Have you any suggestions how best to take this debate forward in the field so that it can best inform policy and practice?

Bibliography

Banks, S. (ed). (1999) *Ethical Issues in Youth Work*. Routledge

Christian, C. (1999) *Youth and Policy, Spirituality in the context of multi-cultural youth work*. The National Youth Agency.

Clapton, T. (1993) *The religious experience and faith development of non-church going young people*. Research thesis.

Fullmi D. & O (2004) *Indian Wisdom 365 days*.Thames and Hudson 2004

Green M. & Heaney C. (2005) *A sense of respect: Interfaith activities for groups of young people*. The National Youth Agency 2005

Griffiths, B. (1994) *Universal Wisdom: A Journey through the sacred wisdom of the world*. Fount 1994

HMI; DES. (1987) Education Observed 6: 'Effective Youth Work'

HMSO 1940: para. 2

HMSO 1944: 10

HMSO 1951

HMSO 1960: 37

Hull, J. (1999) *Youth and Policy*. The National Youth Agency.

Khan, M. G. (2006) *Towards a National Strategy for Muslim Youth Work: Report of the National Conference December 2005*. The National Youth Agency.

Ofsted (1994). *Ofsted Handbook for the Inspection of Schools*

Pimlott, N, Pimlott J, Wiles D. (2005). *Inspire Too*, Frontier Youth Trust Publications. www.fyt.org.uk

Religious Society of Friends (1994) *Quaker Faith and Practice: The Yearly Meeting of the Religious Society of Friends (Quakers) in Britain 1994*

Religious Society of Friends. (2004) *Children and Young People's Report Britain Yearly Meeting*.

Ruth, Sister E. (1985) *Lamps of Fire: Daily Readings with St John of the Cross*. Dartman , Longman and Todd 1985

SCAA (1996) *Education for Adult Life: The Spiritual and Moral Development of Young People.* London.

Tacey, D. (2004) *The Spirituality Revolution*. Brunner. Routledge

The Inter Faith Network for the UK. (2004) *Connect.*

YMCA (1987) *Statement of Purpose YMCA*, 1987:4

Young, K. (1999)(i) *Ethical Issues in Youth Work* ed S. Banks *Youth worker as guide, philosopher and friend*. Routledge 1999

Young, K. (1999)(ii) *The Art of Youth Work,* Russell House Publishing 1999

Youth A Part (1996) Church House Publishing: 1996, p31.

York, National Curriculum Council (1993) *Spiritual and Moral Development – A Discussion Paper*.

Zaehener R.C. (1997) *The Hutchinson Encyclopaedia of Living Faiths*. Hutchinson. London

The following websites were also referred to:

Businessballs (a free online development resource for people)
www.businessballs.com
a website organised and run by Alan Chapman, a speaker, coach and adviser specialising in the ethical and innovative development of people and organisations.

Valdosta State University in Georgia, United States of America.
http://chiron.valdosta.edu/whuitt/col/regsys/maslow.html

Informal education and lifelong learning
www.infed.org – an open, independent and not-for-profit site put together by a small group of educators exploring the theory and practice of informal education and lifelong learning.